ADVENTURES IN CHEAP EATING:

HAWAII

The Comprehensive Guide
to
Righteous Deals
and
Authentic Meals
on
Oahu

MARCH EGERTON

Tsunami Press

Honolulu

Cover Illustration by Christine Joy Pratt
Cover Design by March Egerton and Christine Joy Pratt
Interior Design and Illustrations by March Egerton (Illustrations
on pages 41, 68, 79, and 96 by Sara Holt)

LIBRARY OF CONGRESS CATALOG CARD NUMBER: 93-060643

ISBN: 0-9637709-0-X

FIRST EDITION

TSUNAMI PRESS
P.O. BOX 62197
HONOLULU, HAWAII 96839

To George

For whom good eating and good living
were two halves of the same loaf

INTRODUCTION

When Captain Cook landed in the Hawaiian archipelago in 1788, he promptly named the Islands—much to the surprise of those folks already living here—for his sponsor the Earl of Sandwich, who favored the food article that is his namesake because its portability allowed him to gamble without interruption. Despite not having to contend with the soullessness of modern tourist dining things nonetheless turned out badly for the good Captain, but his unintentional linking of the Isles with a slice of food history was to prove prescient, indeed.

In the ensuing decades Hawaii attracted people from around the globe, all of whom arrived with their distinctive and often ancient culinary habits in tow. Thanks to this multiethnic convergence and a well-documented local love for strapping on the proverbial feedbag, the Islands have proven exceptionally fertile ground for both a perpetuation and melding of cooking styles, in the process taking on the seductive glow of an enormous floating potluck.

Like any other locale, Hawaii is not without its chaff, restaurantwise; and, as is usually the case, those places most worth finding often require the most committed digging. Though the majority of local residents agree that, irrespective of price, few of Oahu's great meals are to be found in Waikiki, many are sadly unaware of the phenomenal array of dining adventures within their grasp. For visitors the situation is all the more dire, and even the most experienced food sleuths can end up thrashing around like a blind dog in a meathouse: agonizingly aware of the nearness of the real deal, yet unable to get at it. That's why a comprehensive reference source—one that cares more about quality and value than it does looks, popularity, promotion or trendiness—is a must.

The vast percentage of eating establishments in *Adventures in Cheap Eating* don't advertise nor do they cater to tourists, and hence they've never found their way into standard travel guides. In more than a few cases, they don't even appear in the phone book. But as someone very wise once said, there is no seasoning as pungent as authenticity, and it is the quest for genuine food at honest prices that drives this book. So say goodbye to your days of hit-or-miss dining, bid a fond farewell to all those expensive disappointments: you're set to discover Hawaii at its finest, a place of extraordinary food, unbelievable bargains, and so many worlds for the choosing.

REQUIRED READING

THE PLEDGE

I have eaten at every establishment discussed in these pages (plus many others that, for one reason or another, proved wanting); and rather saddeningly, to ensure my chastity of judgment I paid for all meals out of my own shallow pocket.

THE WARNING

Few areas of human endeavor are less static than the restaurant business. Though I have attempted to avoid places that seem on the brink of disappearing, I naturally offer no guarantees that you won't, on occasion, roar off in pursuit of the perfect manapua only to find the eatery in question has been replaced by a check-cashing enterprise. Beyond this, be advised that things like addresses, hours (take note that in the case of restaurants with multiple locations I have usually listed *approximate* hours) and (God knows) prices can and do change with the tides. It's why we have telephones.

THE EXPLANATION

So just what do I mean by *cheap*,, anyway? With a handful of notable exceptions, the establishments listed herein offer full meals for under $10 (often way under). Obviously I have allowed for a bit of flex in this area, but in the few instances where I've wholly disregarded the notion (such as Hajjibaba's and Kats Sushi) it's because those dining experiences are sufficiently unique and compelling as to constitute an exceptional bargain in spite of their relative priciness.

THE LINGO

No Plastic means no credit cards are accepted; *Bring Your Own* means you are welcome to bring your own alcoholic beverages, provided of course you don't end up trying to take your shorts off over your head.

That man is richest whose pleasures are the cheapest.
Henry David Thoreau

Why should so vast a national expenditure be left entirely to chance?
Duncan Hines, Adventures in Good Eating (1936)

Then all around from far away across the world
He smelled good things to eat
So he gave up being king of where the wild things are.
Maurice Sendak, Where the Wild Things Are (1963)

AGNES PORTUGUESE BAKE SHOP

35 Kainehe Street   KAILUA
262-5367   6am-6pm Tue-Sun
No Plastic   No Alcohol

Malasadas

✧

Located in a nondescript little building just off the main intersection in downtown Kailua, this is *the* place for malasadas and quality baked goods on the Windward side. From the outside it doesn't appear particularly promising, and the inside, too, has a sort of generic quality about it. Fear not, however; if the setting isn't exactly straight out of Lisbon, the merchandise here is far from ordinary. Take, for example, the traditional Portuguese doughnuts known as malasadas. They're made to order, meaning two things: you'll have to wait a few minutes (no one here's ever in much of a hurry), and they'll be piping hot when they arrive. These are moister than Leonards', with an uncharacteristic hole in the center. Among the very best around, they're about 50 cents apiece and deceptively filling— try them without the traditional hail of granulated sugar. And order only what you can eat right away, as they become mere shadows of their sublime selves after a couple of hours.

Agnes also bakes several different kinds of bread, most notably Portuguese sweet bread (pao doce). Fargoza bread is a delicious variation, thanks to the addition of garlic, onions, cheese, and herbs. Try it with the moderately spicy Portuguese bean soup ($2.25). Whole pies (about $5-$7) are outstanding but usually have to be ordered in advance. Among the dozen or so choices are coconut custard, sweet potato, banana, and mincemeat. The front display area is rife with danishes, turnovers, cinnamon rolls, virtually all costing less than a buck. Check out the fruit pizza and wicked bread pudding. In fact, aside from the cornbread, which is never anything special in these latitudes, you can't go far wrong. ♠

Everybody loves to have things which please the palate put in their way, without trouble or preparation.
Samuel Johnson

AHI'S

Just off Kam Highway

293-5650

No Plastic

KAHUKU

11am-9pm Mon-Sat

Alcohol Served

Seafood

✧

In terms of both miles and mindset, Kahuku is about as far from Honolulu as you can get without leaving Oahu. With neither the banging surf of Sunset, just on the other side of Kahuku Point, nor an official prefab tourist destination like the Polynesian Cultural Center down the road in Laie, Kahuku doesn't get many visitors. This is the country, and Ahi's is one of the only restaurants around—lucky for you, the food's plenty ono.

Hard by the rust-streaked carcass of the old sugar mill, Ahi's is easy to spot thanks to a large sign sitting on a decrepit truck out by the highway. The building itself, meanwhile, seems to exude seafood dining potential, and with its trellises, fishing nets, and tennis balls on the chair feet, the place looks as if it could just as easily be sitting on North Carolina's Outer Banks.

As befits the location, the mood is ultrarelaxed, the staff often barefoot. The menu is straightforward: some sandwiches, a few plate lunch items, and seafood. Almost without exception you'll want to go with the latter, which consists of shrimp dishes plus daily specials like clams, fresh ono, and ahi. For around $7 you can get shrimp cooked one of several ways and served with rice; for an extra two bills you get a complete dinner including salad and sherbet. Shrimp here are from Amorient Aquafarm, an aquaculture establishment about a mile down the road, and they're choice, with flesh that's slightly sweet and unusually dense. Should you crave shellfish in a different guise, excellent alternatives include the pineapple shrimp salad ($7). A beautiful mound of fresh boiled shrimp and succulent fruit served in a pineapple half, it's drizzled with a terrific dressing similar to French only much lighter. Also tasty is the shrimp burger—fried shrimp, fresh and hot, served on a bun with lettuce, onion, tomato, and tartar sauce—a near relation to the ubiquitous poor boy sandwich you find in and around New Orleans. Local-boy owner Ahi Logan is an ardent supporter of the Hawaiian sovereignty movement, but he's hardly a xenophobe. Just check out the exceptional jukebox: everything from Island favorites like Hui Ohana and the Makaha Sons to Louis Armstrong, Johnny Cash (singing "I Walk the Line")—even Bobby Goldsboro, God help us all. ♠

Tourists are free spenders and "eating out" amid country surroundings is the modern vogue—the prevailing recreational fashion.

Duncan Hines, Adventures in Good Eating (1936)

A LITTLE BIT OF SAIGON

1160 Maunakea Street   CHINATOWN
528-3663   10am-10pm Daily
VISA, MC, AMEX   Bring Your Own

Vietnamese

✧

Relatively upscale compared to its neighbors, A Little Bit is roomy, with a plenitude of wood, plants, and pastel hues. A wall-mounted gilded cherub gazes over the proceedings, and paintings by local artists are prominently displayed and available for purchase; some nice, some awful, most all quite large. Things are otherwise pretty routine, but be aware that smokers often flock here, more than a few seeming to treat their gorgeous meals as an afterthought to be consumed between nicotine binges.

The comparative swankiness of the place is reflected in the prices, which exceed those of most Vietnamese eateries by a buck or two per item. The significant exception to this is the $5 pho. Though To Chau around the corner serves the industry standard, Saigon's is in the same league: lean beef, properly cooked noodles, broth that's fresh, clear, and devoid of saltiness or off flavors. The all important side plate of condiments makes for a lovely still life, with licorice-imbued Vietnamese basil, coriander, stinging red chiles, and a heap of turgid sprouts. The seafood soups, though still aspiring to a high level, are smaller and less compelling.

Barring a predisposition to anaphalactic shock, you must try the shrimp and green papaya salad, beguilingly situated on tasty shrimp chips. It's a little steep at $8 (order the regular, as the only thing larger about the large is the plate), but undeniably fine—a light touch on the garlic and chiles, full throttle on the lime and mint. Also delicious are the grilled brochettes of either pork or

3

chicken. With a bed of rice noodles (bun) serving as a palette, they're beautifully presented alongside shredded green mango, carrot, pickled onions, fresh mint, and roasted peanuts. The coconut chicken, meanwhile, is slightly less eye-popping but altogether desirable, thanks to an evening spent soaking in a bath of garlic, fish sauce, and sugar, followed by a brazen dousing of coconut milk.

Tapioca with apple banana is the lone dessert offering and a superb denoument, served hot in a groovy little cereal bowl; not too mushy, not too sweet. Otherwise, be advised that, in a cuisine known for its trippy, semi-solid beverages, A Little Bit stands out. The Che Saigon, touted on the menu as a "bejeweled drink," is too sweet. Number seven is far better, with coconut milk, chipped ice, tapioca and agar agar. Slightly more quaffable offerings include iced tea packed with fresh mint and lime, and fresh-squeezed OJ. ♠

Whiffs of burnt sugar drift into the room, the smell of roasted peanuts, Chinese soups, roast meat, herbs, jasmine, dust, incense, charcoal fires, they carry fire about in baskets here, it's sold in the streets, the smell of the city is the smell of the villages upcountry, the smell of the forest.

Marguerite Duras, The Lover (1985)

AMORIENT AQUAFARM

56-669 Kam Highway   KAHUKU
293-8661   10am-5:30pm Daily
No Plastic   Bring Your Own

Shrimp and Prawns

✧

This roadside operation—known widely as the Prawn Farm—consists of acres of man-made ponds wherein prawns and other shellfish are encouraged to procreate with reckless abandon. The controlled environment is apparently to their liking, as they grow to impressive dimensions before being harvested and A) promptly cooked and sold at the highway stand, or B) shipped out to area restaurants like Ahi's, just down the highway in Kahuku proper.

Prawns are steamed and served straight up, with minimal fanfare or ornament. They are delicious, sweet beyond all imagination, and served with the heads intact. Ditto on the shrimp, which seem more dense than the usual storeboughts and light years beyond anything Red Lobster serves on their best days. These can be had a number of ways: with cocktail sauce ($4), as tempura ($7.50), as a mess of "tails" (this simply means without the heads), or as a shrimp stick, which is 12 to 15 on a skewer for $3.75. Unless you get here early, though, you can usually count on the sticks and the prawns being unavailable. If you want to eat on site there are a few picnic tables where you can look out over the ponds and see the occasional bird or two copping freebies. The deep blue Pacific is just visible in the distance. ♠

All men's gains are the fruits of venturing.
Mardonius (died 479 B.C.), in
Herodotus' *Histories*

ANGELO'S MALASADAS

Roadside at Maili Point   WAIANAE
668-1435   7am-7pm Sat-Sun (usually)
No Plastic   No Alcohol

Malasadas

A while back, Angelo and company made a brief and ulti-mately ill-fated stab at running a full-blown Portuguese restaurant. Though the Portuguese cultural influence is nothing new in Ha-waii, it was the only restaurant of its kind and one which Oahu wasn't able to sustain. Malasadas, however, are a different story, and these folks have fared much better with their roadside stand— basically a makeshift tent, a huge wok-like apparatus filled with bubbling oil, gallons of poofy malasada dough, and some granu-lated sugar for coating the little buggers. For 50 cents a throw you get a work of art, and you can't have them any fresher without earning a trip to the burn unit. These babies are golden brown outside, soft and yeasty inside—beautiful creations to behold. Some-times there's a brief wait, and unfortunately the nearest good cup of coffee is about 20 miles back toward town—but hey, adversity builds character. Keep an eye peeled for other roadside vendors out this way, particularly on weekends, plying huli huli chicken, pasteles, ahi, and so forth. ♠

An immense woman with a glossy picture of a hooked bass leaping the front of her shirt said, "I'm gonna be sick from how much I've ate."

William Least Heat Moon, Blue
Highways (1982)

AOKI'S SHAVE ICE

66-091 Kam Highway   HALEIWA/NORTH SHORE
No Phone   9am-6pm Daily
No Plastic   No Alcohol

Shave Ice

✧

Nowhere is the Hawaiian treat known as shave ice more abundant than on the surf-crazy North Shore. It's available all along Kam Highway in and around Haleiwa, such that it's become somewhat synonymous with the town itself. Without question the most famous place around is Matsumoto's, which has been in business for about 600 years and found its way into virtually every tourist guide, despite the fact that their shave ice isn't even the best in Haleiwa (that would be Miura), much less on Oahu (that would be Waiola Store in Moiliili, hands down).

Aoki's is located just a couple of doors down from Matsumoto's (the two are separated by an exceptionally rickety house of worship—"Experience Jesus at the Haleiwa Assembly of God" reads the hand-lettered sign), and the two are in many ways identical: same slightly chunky ice, same flavors (lemon, banana, pineapple, coconut, and so forth) and gaudily colored syrups, same mammoth servings, same endearingly shabby environs. Aokis's often brisk business is due at least in part to having convincingly imitated their competitor and set up shop close enough to absorb the customers put off by the line at Matsumoto's.

The shave ice here is more like a Mainland snowcone than some in terms of the relatively coarse ice, and the homemade syrups are very sweet and tend to taste alike, with the notable exceptions of the lilikoi and the coffee. Prices run from $1 for a small to $1.80 for a large with vanilla ice cream and sweet azuki beans, which are exceedingly popular among Japanese but sometimes an acquired taste for neophytes. ♠

6

It is not every day that a delicious rice cake falls into the open mouth.

Japanese proverb

AUNTIE PASTO'S

1099 S. Beretania Street
523-8855

VISA, MC

MAKIKI
11am-10:30pm Mon-Th
11am-11pm Fri
4pm-10:30pm Sat-Sun
Alcohol Served

Italian

❖

Unlike most things, Italian food that's both good and affordable doesn't grow on trees in Hawaii. The few places that have identified and sought to fill this niche have often done quite well, and in the estimation of more than a few Oahuans Auntie Pasto's is the island's ranking purveyor of straight-up Italian fare. The freshness of their ingredients is generally impeccable, portions are generous, and the pasta is well cooked, never soggy. As further inducement, with the exception of some rather complicated dishes involving veal shanks virtually everything on the menu is less than $10.

Once you've gotten a table—a feat far more easily accomplished at weekday lunch than weekend dinner—you'll peruse the wall-mounted menu. Prime appetizers include polenta with a light to-mato sauce, and several salads including a mild Caesar, so speak if you want them to up the garlic quotient. Finest of the lot is the tomato with fresh mozza-rella, simple but elegant and only $3.25. Main dishes are pasta or things like veal, eggplant, and chicken—all solid, but at least one person in your party should order the bounteous seafood pasta ($7). While you're deciding you'll be set up with a few veggies and a loaf of excellent bread, crusty and still warm. The wait staff tends to be of the shticky, wisecracking variety, and they do a fine job of taking care of you without hovering.

Desserts include creme brulee and the chilled Sin Pie—fudgy and ultrarich, with a graham cracker crust, whipped cream and

7

toasted almond pieces. Only 12 calories per serving. Parking can be a bear. ♠

Bees are generated from decomposed veal.
Saint Isidore of Seville, 7th century

BABY JOE'S CRUNCHY DOG

4 N. Hotel Street	CHINATOWN
524-3677	10am-1am Daily
AMEX	Alcohol Served

Hot Dogs
✧

Yet another example of the eclectic nature of Chinatown these days, Joe's is an offshoot of a New York-style sandwich joint/tavern, where you can get both a mai tai and a whole Kosher dill pickle, and where sodas are referred to as pop. Sandwiches run in the $4-$6 range, and choices include liverwurst, BLT, and a pretty fair hot pastrami and Swiss. The house specialty though is the hot dogs, referred to for no apparent reason as Crunchy dogs; these are available eight different ways and run $3-$4 including Maui potato chips.

These dogs were voted best-in-show by local newspaper readers a few years back, and they do indeed stand up against any in town. Slender and firm, the all-beef weiners are flown in from New York, then boiled for a few minutes in a secret solution and slipped into what is by Joe's own assessment a rather generic bun. Try the local favorite Korean dog, topped with spicy mustard and a mound of cool, crunchy kim chee—it's an excellent variation on the German sauerkraut theme (which they also offer), only better. Dogs are available at the takeout window to the right of the bar entrance—in true Pavlovian fashion, you'll have to ring the bell for service. For a post-weiner treat, head around the corner to the Sunday Barber Shop (next to Young's Noodle Factory), where a haircut runs $6 and a facial mudpack can be had for $7. Live it up. ♠

Preach not to them what they should eat, but eat as becomes you, and be silent.
Epictetus

BA-LE SANDWICH

150 N. King Street	IWILEI
521-3973	
1154 Fort Street Mall	DOWNTOWN
521-4117	
801 Alakea Street	DOWNTOWN
545-2221	
1199 Dillingham Boulevard	KALIHI
842-0749	
333 Ward Avenue	ALA MOANA
533-2843	
45-1117 Kam Highway	KANEOHE
247-7111	
850 Kam Highway	PEARL CITY
456-1811	
345 Hahani Street	KAILUA
261-2193	
1019 University Avenue	MOILIILI
943-0507	
1620 N. School Street	PALAMA
842-0013	

8am-6pm Daily (more or less)

No Plastic   No Alcohol

Vietnamese Sandwiches

✧

Rather surprisingly in a town so well-endowed with high-quality Vietnamese restaurants, Ba-Le pretty well has the Vietnamese sandwich market cornered. A few places produce slightly superior versions of the form, but Ba-Le is hardly a slouch and they offer the added benefit of proximity.

Vietnamese sandwiches are a marvelous blend of Eastern and Western sensibilities—the crusty French bread (croissants are also available, though somewhat less interesting) and fillings are European-inspired, while the condiments are clear indication of an Asian influence. The end result is a memorable loaf plump with roast chicken or steamed pork, pate or headcheese, all made lively by the addition of pickled carrots and daikon, coriander, and soy sauce. Often these sandwiches are made with indefinable cold cuts (and even then often quite tasty thanks to the accoutrements), but the quality level of ingredients here is quite high. Though Ba-Le offers a

9

few other items like shrimp rolls and green papaya salad (both decent but not extraordinary), sandwiches are clearly the raison d'etre here. Desserts cost a buck and some are quite good, the tapioca and fresh papaya taking top honors. Interiors tend to seem a bit sterile: tile floor, fast-food booths, plenty of plastic. Service is quite swift. ♠

Go as a meat pie, come back as a sandwich.
Malay proverb

BAN ZAI RAHMEN

1103 S. King Street   PAWAA
533-2033   11am-3pm, 6pm-11pm Tue-Sun
No Plastic   No Alcohol

Japanese Noodles

✧

For most locals the soup noodle dish of choice is saimin, which originated in these parts. It's actually a descendant of the Japanese favorite known as rahmen (or ramen), familiar to most Mainlanders only as the underwhelming, six-for-a-dollar Top Ramen they see at Safeway. That stuff is little more than tasteless noodles bobbing in salty, MSG-laced hot water, and it bears little resemblance to the authentic, hearty fare prepared at the likes of Ban Zai and their King Street neighbors Dai Ryu and Sanoya.

At first glance, Banzai looks like something out of an Edward Hopper painting, with 1940's drugstore lettering and immense wall mirrors. Seating consists of a large wrap-around counter with swivel stools, plus a solitary table for two in the corner which has about it a faint air of banishment. The menu's all about Japanese soup noodles, mostly the soft, kinky rahmen noodles, available in several broths including either shoyu or miso, which is prime. Versions range from the simple (chicken), to the vegetarian (a tangle of vegetables and seaweed), to the complex and invigorating Stamina Rahmen. Served in a huge, shallow bowl, it contains bits of just about anything you can think of in terms of meat and vegetables, plus a lightly fried egg; it's touted as being especially beneficial for newlywed males, supplying them with more than adequate amounts of "get up and go." Preliminary research indicates that these folks may be on to something, plus it's damn tasty.

Prices hover in the $5-$6 range, and you won't leave hungry. Besides the obvious appeal of an excellent quick and cheap meal, it's a kick being here when all the seats are filled and there unfolds a strange camraderie among strangers thrown together in close quarters, happily smacking on noodles. ♠

Even though your parents have just died it is still a good thing to rest after eating.
Japanese proverb

BAR-B-Q EAST

540 Kailua Road   KAILUA
262-8457   11am-9pm Mon-Sat
                                                                  5pm-9pm Sun
VISA, MC   Alcohol Served

Japanese/Korean
✧

All commonly accepted notions of scale go by the boards within the confines of this puzzlingly unsung Japanese-Korean eatery. Booths here are expansive and comfortable, the kind you see in faded photos of mafiosos; the platters, meanwhile (the term *plate* simply has no place here), are of the dimensions that cause a serious eater's heart to fibrillate. Meals this size are usually reserved for truck stops and Pratter-Willy support groups, but here you'll find high-quality combination dinners demanding considerable resolve. These run anywhere from about $8 to upwards of $20 if you fancy lobster, but most are in the $10-$12 range; though technically not cheap, they're nonetheless a deal. Pay closest attention to meals offering any or perhaps all of the following: teriyaki beef (tender and gingery, some of the very best around), barbecue chicken, meat jun, tonkatsu, ahi (in any of a number of guises), and tempura (not definitive but quite good, with shrimp the size of a Little League bat). Adding to the absurdity, meals come with rice, miso soup, tsukemono and mac salad.

If cash is tight or you simply don't feel up to the monster grinds, the rest of the menu is quite extensive and there are usually some fine specials like the Hot Spicy Soup for $5.50. This place has

11

been in business for years but it's rarely crowded, and the service is usually efficient. ♠

I had to stand to reach plates across the table, but I intended to do the supper in.

William Least Heat Moon, Blue Highways (1982)

BEA'S PIES

1117 12th Avenue
734-4024
No Plastic

KAIMUKI
6:30am-3pm Tue-Sat
No Alcohol

Pies

✧

Hear the name Bea and you may well have visions of Andy Griffith's girthy, chronically exasperated aunt. The image is only enhanced by the fact that this tiny pie shop is in Kaimuki, a neighborhood about as close to downtown Mayberry as Oahu has to offer. Amid a sea of development, Bea's is the quintessential small business of yore, with a devoted local following and a limited desire to go big time. (Note: They are not affiliated with Bea's Hairstyling down the street.) Bea's has been here for years, and during that time they've garnered a reputation for consistently wonderful pies. Rare is the day when they don't run out of product before the scheduled closing time. As a general rule, you can forget about much in the way of selection past noon. "Sometimes if we're real busy," explains the cheery girl behind the counter, "we'll bake more." On the other hand, they're at least as likely to simply run out early and call it a day, so if you have anything approaching a pathological interest in a specific type of pie, it would behoove you to call ahead—as in a day ahead.

There's just enough space to step inside and ogle the pies on display. Options include apple, blueberry, banana cream, pumpkin custard, peach, apricot. Everything is first-rate, but the custard pies deserve special mention. Besides a virtually unimprovable, thin-yet-sturdy crust, they possess an appealingly smooth egginess capable of rejuvenating pie freaks wounded by encounters with gelatinous pretenders. Accented by hints of nutmeg and vanilla and a surface every so slightly blistered, it's an exceedingly neat pie when allowed to cool. Decor consists of white cardboard pie boxes in every cranny and a sign reading "We Reserve the Right to Refuse Service to <u>Anyone</u>"—so watch your step. Whole pies only, and they cost $7-$8. ♠

Food is the most primitive form of comfort.
Sheilah Graham, A State of Heart
(1972)

BERT'S CAFE

939 McCully Street   McCULLY
No Phone   7am-3pm Mon-Sat
No Plastic   No Alcohol

Plate Lunch
✧

Bert's has all the classic symptoms of an honest-to-God hole-in-the-wall: tiny quarters, no apparent stabs at creating "atmosphere," rock-bottom prices, sporadic hours, no advertising save for a barely discernible sign, and no telephone listing. What it does have, in spades, is the sort of odd charm one finds in places that seem caught in a time warp and obviously don't care. Though there are such unusual plate lunch possibilities as veal patties, corned beef with cabbage, liver and bacon, and creamed tuna, you'll make out far better by exploring the chicken options—more specifically, chicken cutlet, chicken tofu or chicken with stir-fried vegetables. The fried perch is also good, if they happen to have it. In sharp contrast to the dark, catacombish interior, plate lunches here are atypically bright thanks to a tossed salad. They also serve saimin, and if you're in an egg mood there's an unwritten but apparently eternal breakfast special of eggs and rice with some sort of meat (luncheon meat, Spam, Portuguese sausage, corned beef hash, that type of thing) for about $2.75.

Decor is of a motif not yet categorized by the interior decorating establishment, and there is about the place an air of imminent collapse. Booths are freestanding, mismatched, and of sufficient age to recall the term *rumble seat*; behind the counter (piled with papers, magazines, and other miscellanea) are cracked mirrored panels; one corner is devoted to old gambling-style pinball machines (you've got your choice of Laguna Beach or Can Can). In the sunnier, breezier patio area you'll find a huge refrigerator with floral arrangements and leis, a jukebox, a fortune-telling scale (broken, natch), and back issues of *National Geographic* and *Bon Appetit*(!). If Sanford and Son had owned a restaurant, it would have looked like this. ♠

Life is too short to stuff a mushroom.
Shirley Conran, Superwoman
(1975)

BO LAI

1117 S King Street

524-9312

VISA, MC

PAWAA

10:30am-10pm Mon-Sat

5pm-9pm Sun

Bring Your Own

Cantonese

✧

Bo Lai is a small, unpretentious joint primarily serving Cantonese fare, though they make the occasional foray into the spicier cuisines of China's other provinces. Much menu space is devoted to standards like pepper salt shrimp (quite good but not the item of choice if you're feeling especially hungry), deep-fried stuffed tofu, and chicken with black bean sauce. There are also a goodly number of noodle options. The Shanghai chow mein is among the finest of these, while the mu shu chicken is an impressive variation on the traditional pork favorite. They offer an unusual version of the omnipresent eggplant with garlic sauce, heavy on the bamboo shoots and minus the tangy, slightly caramelized effect one often finds. Timid palates can order without compunction, as even traditionally fiery dishes like kung pao chicken exhibit the Cantonese aversion to chiles. Portions are adequate but not enormous, so you may want to start with an order of crispy gau gee, freshly cooked and served with sweet and sour dipping sauce.

There are only a few tables and large groups frequently commandeer one side of the restaurant; nonetheless, there's rarely a wait. Attempts at ambience are nominal—a tile floor, clips of favorable restaurant reviews posted here and there. As is often the case with Chinese eateries, the walls are plastered with signs declaring specials of one sort or another; brief study will reveal that they basically repeat those listed on the menu. Prices are pretty much what you'd expect, with virtually everything in the $5-$8 range. The staff can be a jot on the quirky side. ♠

Decapitation is a gruesome affair but I am condemned to die that way...Be sure not to forget to eat dried bean curd with fried peanuts. The two give you the taste of the best ham.

Chin Sheng-Tan, instructions to his son in his will (17th century)

BUBBIE'S

1010 University Avenue   MOILIILI
949-8984   12pm-12am Mon-Th
                                   12pm-1am Fri-Sat
                                12pm-11:30pm Sun
No Plastic   No Alcohol

Ice Cream
✧

Just down the hill from the University of Hawaii, Bubbie's has the hokey, neo-antiquated look of a mainland Swensen's. But despite the heartland complexion, their product is made locally and it's excellent. The flavor list, though not the largest in town, changes on a fairly regular basis. Generally, you'll do right by opting for their exotic blends: white chocolate-macadamia and papaya-ginger are but a couple of winners that make impressive use of Island ingredients. The latter contains no milk—a sort of sorbet almost crumbly in texture (they won't serve it in cones), but subtle and absolutely fantastic. Bubbie's displays a knack for converting popular beverages into lickable form—the mulled apple cider packs the cinnamon twang of the genuine article, and the green tea is likewise authentic. For those fans of the form who find Dave's green tea overpowering, Bubbies' is probably what you're after.

Portions are hefty and a single scoop runs around two bucks, a double $3 and change (for a whopping 11 ounces of ice cream). They actually offer five different sizes, the smallest of which is listed on the chalkboard as Fetal Dip—a questionable choice of nomenclature, perhaps, but nothing compared to the ice cream pies and fudgy concoctions with names like Multiple Orgasm, Come Here Little Girl..., and the simultaneously repulsive and irresistible

15

Functioning Prostate. These are rich to the point of being, from a nutritional standpoint, akin to ingesting straight butter—but then decadence isn't something to be done halfway. Bubbie's is often crowded, thanks in part to the proximity of the Varsity theaters, which offer Hawaii's best selection of slightly offbeat films while assiduously avoiding anything along the McCauley Culkin-Schwarzenegger axis. ♠

The effect of eating too much lettuce is "soporific."
Beatrix Potter, Flopsy Bunnies

BUDDHIST VEGETARIAN RESTAURANT

100 N. Beretania Street   CHINATOWN
532-1868   10:30am-2pm, 5:30pm-10pm Mon-Fri
                                                      8am-2pm, 5:30pm-10pm Sat-Sun
VISA, MC, AMEX   Alcohol Served

Dim Sum
✧

Though strict vegetarians, Buddhist monks have long sought to approximate the taste, texture and appearance of animal flesh by the often ingenious manipulation of wheat gluten and bean curd. While other Chinese eateries offer these so called mock meats, Buddhist is the only one trafficking in them exclusively. The dining room here is bright and cheerful, if a bit ster- ile, and aside from various statuettes of well-fed Buddhas, the most salient at- mospheric feature is a chandelier of such grand, sparkly di- mensions as to make one wonder if Liberace merely faked his own death and is now in the restaurant biz. At any rate the staff, which even dur- ing busy periods seems to enjoy a one-to-one ratio with patrons, is extremely eager to please.

The tea served here is unusual, much earthier than the typical brew—connoisseurs may find it resembles a variety called pu-ehr, while the less urbane have been heard to exclaim that it tastes a bit like, well, dirt. Sip as you scan the menu, which includes some interesting choices—all of them Cantonese—and runs the range from soups such as Eight Treasures ($7) to some very fine tofu dishes ($6.50-$8). Other selections are the peculiar stir-fried broccoli with elm fungus and the lovely vegetables and mushrooms with pine nuts in a taro basket (around $8). Noodle dishes are ample but tend in the direction of oiliness. Desserts include that down-home favorite, green bean soup.

Though the prices are a trifle out of line for a meat-free establishment, Buddhist is especially worth a visit for any serious vegetarian who enjoys the luxury of being free to choose from an entire menu that's widely varied and creatively conceived. Buddhist is also home to Hawaii's only meatless dim sum. ♠

Every vegetarian knows what a pig looks like.
Chinese proverb

BUENO NALO

41-865 Kalanianaole Highway   WAIMANALO
259-7186   11:30am-9pm Daily
No Plastic   Bring Your Own

Mexican
✧

Waimanalo is noteworthy for a number of reasons—it was the home of slack key legend Gabby Pahinui, it has the sort of uncrowded, picture-postcard beaches that make Waikiki seem like a bad joke, *and* it's where you'll find one of the most eclectic Mexican joints on the island.

Over the years, Bueno Nalo has had an uneven existence—it used to be great before dropping off precipitously, and now it's back on track. Though you'll still find Oahu's best Mexican food down the road at El Charro Avitia, the grinds here are certainly adequate—especially by Hawaii standards—and the atmosphere is terrific. Housed in a pleasantly crumbled building, the decor is a study in Mexicano motifs, along with some impressive artworks that are available for purchase. And observe, please, the regal matador done in black velvet, the high shelf crammed with votives, Jesuses, and assorted religious paraphernalia. Throw in a selection of sombreros, mariachi instruments, mismatched chairs, beer bottles, and the album cover of *Les Baxter's Wild Guitars*, and you get the feeling the Border Patrol could bust in any second.

Ah yes, the food. Chips and salsa are good here, and they buck the trend toward charging for extras. Soft corn tortillas work well for the tacos (around $6 for three—guacamole or chicken are a go, but skip the fish version), but they make an unsatisfactory foundation for the rather immense tostadas. If you want crispy, go for the $7-$8 chimichangas instead (big as your forearm and served seven different ways). They also have burritos, tamales, and enchiladas. The beans are free of animal products, and the desserts—flan and sopapillas—are good but a little pricey. Just as well, because you probably won't have room anyway. ♠

I've had some good, and I've had some bad.
Peter Watson, age 10, on chili
(circa 1970)

CAFE HALEIWA

66-460 Kam Hwy   HALEIWA/NORTH SHORE
637-5516   6am-2pm Mon-Fri
                                                 7am-2pm Sat-Sun
No Plastic   Bring Your Own

Breakfast
✦

Given Oahu's varietal abundance of terrific eats, I'm hard-pressed to explain the island's relative dearth of inexpensive yet memorable breakfast outlets. With the exception of Eggs 'n Things (and even there you have to know what to order), Waikiki is a particularly sad wasteland, rife with Chinese restaurants offering $1.99 eggs-and-pancakes specials—a spectacle of cross-cultural befuddlement rarely worth crossing the street. By contrast, this groovy surfer hangout serves up a morning meal that constitutes reason enough for traversing the entire island.

Breakfast is what it's all about here, and early risers and hard-core insomniacs will find the aforementioned eggs and flapjacks special, done up proper and referred to as the Dawn Patrol. Otherwise, there's plenty to choose from including stout omelettes, superb pancakes and French toast, and the Off the Lip (eggs with your choice of ham, bacon, Canadian bacon, links, Portuguese sausage, turkey or the commendable seven-veggie saute, plus home fries, rice, or beans, and toast or tortillas). In addition there are usually a few daily specials, with fresh mahi making frequent appearances. The coffee is passable and refills are attentively provided by bare-midriffed waitresses. Prices hover in the $5 range.

Atmosphere is, not surprisingly, surfing-inspired. Posters and photos pay homage to the sport of kings, and the relaxed interior is otherwise characterized by wood, plants, and tunes that thoroughly cover the British Invasion-Hendrix-Motown territory. Parking, such as it is, is over by the dumpster and out back between the banana grove and the enormous mango tree; expect a brief wait most mornings, particularly if the surf's up. And that little blue shack with the crescent moon in the door is the bathroom. Hang ten. ♠

Eat breakfast like a king, lunch like a prince, and dinner like a pauper.
Adelle Davis, Let's Eat Right to Keep Fit (1954)

CALIFORNIA PIZZA KITCHEN

4211 Kahala Mall	KAHALA
737-9446	
1910 Ala Moana Boulevard	WAIKIKI
955-5161	
Pearlridge Shopping Center	AIEA
487-7741	
11am-10:30pm Mon-Th	11am-11pm Fri-Sun
	(hours vary slightly)
VISA, MC, AMEX	Alcohol Served

California Cuisine

Based on more bad experiences than I have any desire to recount, I'm always a bit skeptical of things chain-related: chain-smokers, chain letters, and most definitely chain restaurants, which have an irritating tendency to make much ado over nothing and charge too much in the process. However, every so often I have to admit an exception to this mostly flawless way of thinking. CPKs are purveyors of West Coast/California cuisine—a blending of distinctive and often unlikely ingredients to create new and occasion-

19

ally dazzling variations on traditional dishes. Pizza offerings include rosemary chicken-potato and Santa Fe chicken; pasta dishes are likewise eclectic, employing such novel ingredients as tequila and Thai peanut sauce to wonderful effect. They make a big point of letting you know the pizzas (individual-sized and costing $8-$10) are baked in coal-fired ovens; regardless of whether or not you're mightily impressed by this, their pies are quite fine, though not particularly reminiscent of traditional pizza as both tomato sauce and cheese are often absent. Salads here are quite nice as well, especially the copious Greek version, laced with olives and goat cheese. Desserts run toward the exotic, and the $5 tiramisu (cream cheese, Marsala custard and lady fingers, with the added consequence of espresso, rum and bittersweet chocolate) is worth it if you have help. In true self-effacing chain restaurant fashion, CPK offers a wide selection of items, from aprons to canvas tote bags, all emblazoned with the company logo. Hooray. ♠

Work before eating, rest after eating. Eat not ravenously, filling the mouth gulp after gulp without breathing space.

Maimonides

CAMPBELL CHINESE RESTAURANT

3122 Castle Street   KAPAHULU
732-3017   11am-9pm Wed-Mon
No Plastic   Bring Your Own

Cantonese

Tucked away just off Kapahulu Avenue, this 8-year-old establishment offers excellent Cantonese fare served up in an atmosphere more reminiscent of an Elk's Lodge than anything from the South of China. Tile floor, Naugahyde chairs, veneer tables, artworks as hideous as they are immense—you get the idea.

The decor and the dreary appellation notwithstanding, the food here is of a high caliber and extremely affordable. Service is exceptionally cheerful, the hot tea tasty and reassuring, the portions steadfastly gargantuan. The soups in particular—prominently featured along with noodle dishes of all stripes—are loaded with hunks of duck and other edible trinkets and served in a bowl large enough for an impromptu baptism. Most are under $5.

The list of seafood offerings runs well into double digits, in addition to which there's usually some sort of special depending on what's handy. Though usually the kind of thing you want to avoid, the standard lunch plate here is a $4.25 revelation: chow mein with freshly cooked vegetables and sliced pork, bright red char siu, sweet and sour spareribs, rice, fried shrimp and won tons. A mound of food, plain and simple. Campbell is within walking distance of Waikiki and in close proximity to Kapiolani Park, the zoo, Diamond Head. ♠

It is better to let the man wait for his soup than to let the soup wait for the man.
Chinese proverb

CATANIA RISTORANTE ITALIANO

2671 S. King Street	MOILIILI
949-3545	5pm-10pm Tue-Sun
VISA, MC	Bring Your Own ($1.50 corkage fee)

Italian
✧

The food here is well worth overcoming any distracting subconscious tendency to read the name as Catatonia. There are only nine tables and they don't take reservations, so a short wait is not unlikely. This diminutiveness begets a setting that's intimate and romantic, yet relatively free of affectation or adornment. Lighting is subtle and indirect, quite suitable for nuzzling and cross-table feeding. Which brings us to the food: appetizers include prosciutto and melon and a pretty fair antipasto for two (both around $5); the carpaccio (thin-sliced raw steak served with olive oil and capers) is another good bet. The salads aren't as reliable, but loading up on preliminaries isn't advised anyway as entrees are often monstrous. They come in two sizes, regular and small ($2 less), the latter ample for most anyone who isn't bucking for a job as Rush Limbaugh's stunt double.

Quality is high among the pasta and seafood dishes—try the absurdly rich fettucini carbonara, the eggplant parmigiana served over linguine (both about $10/regular), or the shrimp saltimbocca ($12/regular), made with eggplant, mozzarella, prosciutto, mushrooms, butter and white wine. The scallops alla veneziana features bivalves in a heady tomato sauce augmented by bacon, olive oil, garlic and fresh basil. Otherwise there's calamari and plenty of chicken and veal in numerous milieus—Marsala, piccata, cacciatore. The chefs can be a little timid with the spices, so make your preferences known. If you can manage, desserts are delicious and cheap ($3 or less). Try the fresh fruit with homemade rum sauce and whipped cream or the spiffy zabaglioni, a whipped custard made with sweet Marsala wine. ♠

No man is lonely while eating spaghetti—it requires too much attention.
Christopher Morley

CHAN'S

2600 S. King Street   MOILIILI
949-1188/949-1093   10:30am-11:30pm Daily
VISA, MC, AMEX   Alcohol Served

Dim Sum
✧

When it comes to dim sum, Chan's is strictly small-time in comparison with its competitors. While establishments like Yong Sing and China House woo the tea-and-dumplings crowd with massive selections served in an almost auditorium-like setting, Chan's keeps things pretty simple. The interior is cozy, comfortable and quite pink; the staff works the room with rolling steam wagons, offering up char siu manapua, shumai, chicken look fun rolls, and so forth. As at most dim sum houses the crew does their best to push whatever they happen to be carrying at the moment (at many places they are paid on commission)—take your time, though, as some items here are only so-so. Generally speaking, the baked items are nothing to wake the neighbors over; if you want to do yourself right, order any and all of the steamed seafood items. Among these are the terrific har gau (shrimp in translucent dough) and the absolutely stellar hai suen gau (minced seafood packed with chopped coriander in a small dumpling), easily one of the best dim sum items in all of Hawaii. Also check out the steamed mochi rice pouch and the various goodies wrapped in spongy fried bean curd. Most prices run in the $1.50-$3 range, and Chan's also offers a full menu of Cantonese standards which are generally quite reliable. ♠

We [the Chinese] eat food for its texture, the elastic or crisp effect it has on our teeth, as well as for fragrance, flavor and color.
Lin Yutang

CHAO PHYA THAI

Windward City Shopping Center   KANEOHE
235-3555   11am-2pm, 5pm-9pm Mon-Sat
                                                              /5pm9pm Sun
VISA, MC   Bring Your Own

Thai
✧

Though Vietnamese food is the more omnipresent and consistent Southeast Asian cuisine in these parts, the recent American mania for Thai meals has by no means bypassed the Islands. And while Honolulu can boast of numerous Thai eateries (of widely varying quality), the Windward coast hasn't seen much Thai action and Chao Phya remains one of the lone outposts on the rainy side of the pali. Perhaps galled by the celebrity-worship cheesiness of Keo's, they bill themselves as "a totally unpretentious Thai restaurant," which translates into comfortable rattan chairs, a bright two-wall jungle mural, and zero framed photos of the proprietors glad-handing it with Dionne Warwick's personal psychic. The food here is always reliable and at times excellent, with a pronounced emphasis on curries. Their flair for the atypical shows from the first course. The spring rolls, for example, are loaded with ground beef, potatoes, green peas and onion—similar to an Indian somosa. Of the salads, the Chao Phya's the one to get: it's made with lettuce, assorted vegetables, meat and shrimp, all treated to a cool shower of sweet-and-sour dressing of coconut/peanut origins.

Other attempts at sweet-and-sour are less successful and generally rate second to any of the aforementioned curries (red, yellow, or green), which are both sizable and complex. Other stirring ventures are the garlic pork (or shrimp) and the pad thai, cryptically listed here as Newspaper Noodles. With the exception of a few seafood items, everything's in the $6 range, and a large bowl of sticky rice can be had for a $2 bill. Thai iced coffees are very inexpensive at $1.25, though for my money they don't compare with the Vietnamese rendition. Unless your heart is set racing by the phrase "Julio Iglesias World Tour," the music will not impress you. ♠

The discovery of a new dish does more for the happiness of a man than the discovery of a star.
Brillat Savarin

CHAR HUNG SUT

64 N. Pauahi Street   CHINATOWN
538-3335   5:30am-2pm Wed-Mon
No Plastic   No Alcohol

Manapua
✧

It is when standing in places like Char Hung Sut that Hawaii seems most like another country. It's a dank little shop where the sustained flurry of activity alternately suggests choreography and chaos, where everything is done by hand and English fluency is not always of much benefit. Despite the austere surroundings and a lack of even the most cursory advertising, lines are a virtual certainty. Over the course of nearly half a century word has a way spreading, and Char Hung Sut is famous for making some of the finest manapua and dim sum snacks this side of Hong Kong.

The shop is tiny, stacked from concrete floor to ceiling with paper boxes and round metal steam trays. The list of offerings is fittingly minimal—manapua made with either char siu, taro or black sugar (60 cents), and a few smaller items like shumai (referred to locally as pork hash) and translucent half moons stuffed with minced pork and vegetables(perhaps their best item and all of 35 cents apiece). Everything is continually made fresh before your eyes by the women at the long wooden table, who sit surrounded by mounds of dough and filling. Methodically they roll and stuff, roll and cut, chatting in Chinese and eyeing the clientele. Many have probably made a million or more of the little dumplings in their careers. Manapua are the definitive cheap meal in Hawaii, and Char Hung

 Sut's are simply beyond reproach. They are larger than most, warm, puffy and slightly resilient, with the perfect ratio of filling to dough. Only with considerable difficulty will you be able to down more than three—two usually does the trick. They often run out of most everything by noon or so, sometimes earlier. It's takeout only. ♠

"Nearly eleven o'clock," said Pooh happily. "You're just in time for a smackerel of something."
A. A. Milne, The House at Pooh Corner

CHIANG MAI

2239 S. King Street
941-1151

VISA, MC, AMEX

MOILIILI
11am-2pm, 5:30pm-9:45pm Mon-Fri
5:30pm-9:45pm Sat-Sun
Alcohol Served

Thai
✧

The atmosphere at this popular eatery is pleasant and cozy, with exposed beams and silently spinning fans overhead; the subdued lighting (colored parasols cover each bulb) is conducive to pre-meal amorousness. Plants abound, further fostering a feeling of privacy and intimacy in what is actually a pretty cramped place. The off-white walls are peculiarly textured, like something you might use to practice your rock-climbing moves. White tablecloths and fresh flowers are de rigeur, and the music selection proves conclusively that tunes like "Have You Never Been Mellow?" sound just as bad with Thai lyrics.

Thai appetizers are always a kick, and the modest entree portions virtually demand them here. The pleasantly resilient tod mun pla (deep-fried fish cakes made with bits of hot chile and minced string bean) and the stuffed Chiang Mai wings are both excellent. The latter are described as "a conversation piece"—something to keep in mind if your date's going poorly. Soup making is nothing short of an art form in Thailand, and Chiang Mai's Spicy Chicken (with the zip of kaffir lime leaves) and Royal Chicken (featuring coconut milk and pleasantly bulbous straw mushrooms) are both nice choices for about $6. At soup time someone invariably chomps down on a bark-like material somewhat redolent of sarsaparilla. That's sumac root—don't eat it.

With the exception of the seafood dishes, which are underwhelming and overpriced, entrees are reliable but often a bit puny. The pad thai ($5.50) is quite tasty, and there are three kinds of fried rice. Best of the curries is the green version; made with eggplant, chiles and sweet basil, it's hot enough to start some trouble. The Evil Beef and Evil Chicken (around $6) are other solid options. Dessert is either tapioca or apple banana in warm coconut milk—both delicious, and, though not indicated on the menu, available as a combo ($2). Bring a snack. ♠

More die in the United States of too much food than too little.

John Kenneth Galbraith

CHINA HOUSE

1349 Kapiolani Boulevard
949-6622
VISA, MC

ALA MOANA
10am-9pm Daily
Alcohol Served

Dim Sum

✧

Over the years, China House has gained a deserved reputation for serving some of the choicest dim sum in Hawaii. And while they also offer a complete menu—after all, dim sum is only served until 2 p.m.—dumplings and the like remain their justifiable claim to fame. The bright red building looks convincingly like an elaborate Chinese temple; the interior is likewise attractive and comfortable, too, with carpet, intricate wood paneling, painted screens, partitions, and relief art. There's also a wonderfully ornate ceiling which helps counterbalance the cavernous feel inevitable with a restaurant of this magnitude (they must have at least 100 tables).

Simply put, dim sum here is an experience not to be missed. They have nearly 40 varieties, all lovingly depicted on a picture menu that comes in quite handy, particularly if you don't speak Chinese. Though the selection can seem daunting, order with confidence as everything is superb. For sweets try the Malayan cake, the lotus sugar bao, or the crispy egg cream bao (baked buns filled with coconut egg custard); savory items to watch for include the pan-fried turnip cake, boneless chicken bao, har gau (half moons fat with shrimp—fantastic), chicken and chive gau, shrimp salad goh, deep-fried squid, duck web with mushrooms, and the attache-sized mochi rice chicken pouch, which is steamed in banana leaf and way delicious. As per usual, condiments are basic—shoyu and hot Chinese mustard, to be mixed and used as a universal dipping sauce.

Whereas some places price their dim sum by the piece, a China House order is usually two or three units, with most prices hovering around $2-$3. Your tally will be kept by one of the many staff, easily recognized by their matching red tops and quick feet. Dim sum aside, you may want to try the noodles or perhaps the hot pots, listed on the menu as casseroles. Most items are around $8, but if you've got bucks to burn they have some pricier items worth checking out, like shredded steak in a fried taro nest ($11.50), lobster with cashew nuts ($22), and steamed fresh Island fish. They're also big into both shark's fin and bird's nest soups, and you can even get them in combination ($20). ♠

He whose belly is full believes not him who is fasting.
Chinese proverb

CHINA INN

66-250 Kam Highway
637-5876
VISA, MC

HALEIWA/NORTH SHORE
9am-10pm Tue-Sun
Bring Your Own

Cantonese/Szechuan

✧

Chinese food is still a relatively scarce commodity on the North Shore, as is for that matter Asian food of any dimension. The food gods must be smiling on this sparsely populated, unassuming sector of Oahu, however, for despite the lack of citizenry it has more than its share of good eats, and China Inn rates as something of a jewel.

Sitting back from the highway in a low-key shopping center, China Inn shows little outward promise. Venture inside, though, and you'll find some of the best Chinese food for miles—fresh, hot, spicy, as tasty as they are handsome. Combination plates offer rice or chow mein and a choice of one to three entrees, with prices starting at around $3. Selection varies, but it's all high-grade. Usually available are spicy chicken, tangy and substantial sesame chicken, sweet-and-sour shrimp (for that matter sweet-and-sour anything is a sure bet here), and roast duck. Also keep an eye out for tofu eggplant, bitter melon with pork, and some of the best chicken with broccoli in Hawaii.

The interior here is no more exciting than the exterior: a half dozen tables, a few surfing posters, and that's about it. The outdoor seating is much more pleasant, and after you've eaten step around the corner to watch the folks at North Shore Glass blowing in the parking lot. A few doors the other direction is a shop dealing in tropical birds whose beauty is matched only by their verboseness— keep a sharp eye on any shiny objects you hold dear. Down at the far end of the complex is the Coffee Gallery, one of the best spots on the island for a cup of hot and black. ♠

An inn-keeper does not object to greedy appetites.
Chinese proverb

CHOI'S YAKINIKU

1736 Kapiolani Boulevard
947-6861
VISA, MC

ALA MOANA
10:30am-10pm Daily
Alcohol Served

Korean
✧

No point in mincing words: from the outside, Choi's looks like hell. Situated at one end of a peculiar, oblong building with peeling beige paint, it has no windows, a "COCKTAILS" sign above the door, and a general air of seediness that suggests the potential for activities of an unsavory nature.

Once inside, though, you'll discover a tidy Korean restaurant not unlike numerous others around town. A family place, in fact, with booths hugging the curved walls in such a way that the overall effect, particularly given the absence of sunlight, is that of dining in the prow of a ship. Koreans are big into booths, and Choi's has nothing but: brown leatherette numbers, some vast enough for 10 people, with white Formica tables. Decor consists of electric beer signs, thrift store art (heavy on oceans and mountains), and a banner touting the popular Korean liquor Jinro Soju (50 proof) with the slogan, "Tastefully Light, Socially Right."

As you sip your roasted barley tea and scan the menu, you'll probably notice items like the beef tongue yakiniku and "Small

Intestine Soup, hot and spicy." Though you may not order them, they're clear indication that a Choi's repast is unflinchingly authentic. Soups include man doo, oxtail, and dried fish versions. From the stew list, try the blue crab or the kim chee stew, with beef or pork, daikon, hunks of tofu, fresh mushrooms, green onions, and kim chee so hot it comes perilously close to a poor man's tonsillectomy. Both soups and stews come in ancient-looking black cauldrons that resemble something dredged up from the *Andria Doria*; after delivery the con- tents continue boiling in an almost pre- ternatural fashion for several minutes. Plan on some serious sweating if you go this route, but it really is first class stuff. Otherwise go for the noodles, which are handmade buckwheat strands served with vegetables. Mighty delicious.

Prices here—most everything is in the $6.50-$10 range—are a notch above a Korean barbecue joint, but well worth it. Besides rice, meals are accompanied by multiple side dishes, all of impeccable quality—kim chee, watercress sprinkled with sesame seeds, crisp and mild cucumbers, seaweed, and chewy slivers of fried tofu soaked in a soy-ginger marinade. ♠

Even a gentleman with a beard three feet long cannot do without eating.
Korean proverb

CHUN WAH KAM NOODLE FACTORY

505 Kalihi Street   KALIHI
841-5303   7am-4pm Mon-Sat
                                             7am-12pm Sun
No Plastic   No Alcohol
Chinese Noodles/Manapua
✧

Unlike other noodle factories around town, especially those in Chinatown, Chun Wah Kam is housed in a relatively new-looking building; also unlike most noodle shops, they serve takeout. The menu is fairly limited, and $3.60 buys you one entree with either fried rice or noodles—one guess as to which you should order. The

29

chow mein is excellent—sturdy, never mushy, laced with shredded cabbage, onions, and carrots—and the wide and chewy chow fun better still. Entrees like broccoli beef and ung choy are decent if unspectacular, and it's definitely better to get here toward the early part of the day as they tend to let things sit (not to mention they run out of chow fun). Portions are very generous; order the succulent oyster chicken, for example, and you'll receive the better part of half a bird, plus an out-and-out hillock of noodles. It's takeout only, and the atmosphere is characterized by bags of cabbage outside the door, tight parking, and glimpses of the noodle area, the floor dusted with flour. A few dim sum items are also offered: half moons are fine but tend to disappear early and the manapua (70 cents) are substantial if not quite to the level of Char Hung Sut—no shame in that. Both the char siu and shoyu chicken versions are excellent and swollen with filling. ♠

Always entertain a teacher with minced meats, fish, and shrimp.

Chinese proverb

CIAO NOW

1120 Maunakea Street   CHINATOWN
521-1487   10am-4:30pm Daily
No Plastic   No Alcohol

Italian

✧

Like every other food stall in the Maunakea Marketplace, Ciao Now is takeout only and they close by mid-afternoon; unlike their neighbors, though, they offer pizza and pasta instead of various and sundry Asiatic delights. Pizza they sell whole or by the hefty slice (about $2), and the two to watch for are the deep-dish vegetarian (made with whatever looks best in the neighboring groceries) and the Snow White pie—a meatless, tomatoless extravaganza made with three kinds of cheese. Sandwiches (dirt cheap at $2.95) are served on homemade sourdough with a number of fillings, the best of which is probably the eggplant parmigiana. Other dishes to remember are the polenta and the linguini with freshly made clam sauce—either white or red, both are strong. There are also usually specials like potato, onion and cheese casserole, made with both white and sweet potatoes. Vegetarians are well-provided for here, and virtually everything is $6 or less. Keep in mind that this is a very small operation and hence prone to running out of some items rather quickly; other selections may be listed but unavailable on a given day, subject to fits of whimsy. Top things off with a slice of the groovy apple pie pizza, made with cinnamon, ricotta cheese, and honey, not necessarily in that order. ♠

Food is an important part of a balanced diet.
Fran Leibowitz, Metropolitan Life
(1978)

C-MUI CENTER

77 S. Pauahi Street
536-4712

No Plastic

DOWNTOWN
9:30am-5pm Mon-Fri
9:30am-3pm Sat
No Alcohol

Crack Seed
✧

Touting itself as "your one stop snack shop," C-Mui Center has amassed quite a loyal following after more than 30 years of doing their part to satisfy Hawaii's voracious demand for crack seed and related snacks. Crack seed shops like this one are the quintessential mom-and-pop operation, and the last quarter century of rampant inflation in the Islands hasn't been particularly kind to them. But while others have been dropping like flies (or remaining in business by cutting corners on their product), C-Mui has stayed the course and prospered, at least in part because their crack seed is the match of any around.

Just off the Fort Street Mall across from an exotic nightspot called Club Top Gun, this narrow shop is lined on both sides with the trademark glass jars full of snacks—around 70 kinds in all. Besides the myriad versions of preserved plum (li hing mui), there's a wide and excellent variety of mochi crunch, plus more esoteric items like dried scallops. Try the sweet-sour cherries, and if you go in for more full-on sourness, the lime balls (actually dried kum-

31

quats) will have you sucking in your cheeks for the rest of the afternoon. Also irresistible are the preserved olives, resembling the storebought kind only in shape (these are sometimes referred to in the crack seed biz as "footballs"). They are sweet and salty, much like the ubiquitous plums, but with a crunchy texture similar to preserved mango. Something of a specialty here are the kam cho plums, peaches and apricots. These are dark and coated with light flakes, the overriding flavor being that of licorice. Check 'em out. ♠

After the bitter comes the sweet.
Chinese proverb

COFFEE GALLERY

66-250 Kam Highway   HALEIWA/NORTH SHORE
637-5571   6am-9pm Sun-Th
                                                           6am-11pm Fri-Sat
VISA, MC, AMEX   No Alcohol

Coffeehouse
✧

For my money at least, this is the coolest coffee house in Hawaii. Besides serving a nice cup of mud and some memorable food items, they have the sort of relaxed, comfortable environs that make you feel like hanging out, reading a book, writing a letter, playing kanasta, scanning the want ads, whatever.

Throughout the shop are bags of coffee in flavors ranging from Kona to hazelnut, amaretto to Girl Scout Cookie, as well as large burlap sacks of unroasted beans from around the world—Ethiopia, Mexico, Columbia, Kenya, Indonesia. Several flavors and blends are brewing at any given time, and bean quality is generally quite high. Best of all, the flavors of the day run $1 for a 12-ounce cup (20 ounces if you get it iced).

On the edible side, they offer sandwiches as well as lox and bagels and a decent garden burger. Baked goods—chocolate date scones, blueberry crumbcake, brownies, cookies, muffins—are appetizing and run around $2, with some being suitable for vegans. There's also some sort of dinner offering, usually on the light side—vegetarian tostadas, soup, that type of thing. Breakfast is the meal of choice here: waffles run $5-$6 and come topped with papaya and bananas, and there's also a papaya boat filled with yogurt and granola. Wash them down with fresh wheat grass juice or carrot juice.

Besides good coffee and good food, Coffee Gallery has character. There are original artworks all around, split coffee sacks on the ceiling, and a terrific screened lanai furnished with mismatched wooden tables and chairs. Wafting in from the Birds of Aloha shop next door are the squawkings of mischief-minded macaws and cockatiels. ♠

Good coffee should be black like the devil, hot like hell, and sweet like a kiss.

Hungarian proverb

COFFEELINE

1810 University Avenue
947-1615
No Plastic

UNIVERSITY
8am-8pm Mon-Fri
No Alcohol

Coffeehouse
✧

Though the banner out front proudly proclaims this grungy, laid-back establishment a "Free Thought Zone," don't be misled: This is PC territory, as in Politically Correct, and you can count on a far friendlier reception if your audible musings lean more in the direction of Gloria Steinem than, say, Phyllis Schlafly.

Located in the YWCA building across from the University of Hawaii's main campus, the atmosphere here consists of hand-decorated furniture, some potted plants, Malcolm X posters, and announcements for various and sundry empowerment meetings. The mood is quite relaxed, and this is an excellent place to read, chat, or strum a guitar. They offer counter service only, and the kitchen is really no more elaborate than what's found in the typical home. Hence, the menu is very basic—a vegetarian soup of the day (yea on the African groundnut or the lentil, nay on the curry), and sandwiches (egg salad, tofu, cheese) topped with vegetables.

33

Breadwise, opt for the French loaf if they have it. There are a few baked goods which are decent but not the kind of thing to justify a trip across the pali. The coffee drinks are usually OK, and cold beverages are in the fridge to your left. Bring a book or bring a friend. Bay doves often fly in looking for handouts, as does the occasional white Rasta. ♠

If you want to improve your understanding, drink coffee.

Sydney Smith

COFFEE MANOA

Manoa Marketplace
988-5113

MANOA
7am-9pm Mon-Fri
8am-5pm Sat-Sun

AMEX

No Alcohol

Coffeehouse

✧

This is one of the big kahunas in Honolulu's recent coffeehouse proliferation, and one of the best. The inside is understated and attractive, with mirrors, parquet flooring, dark wood counters, and ceiling fans. There are tables inside and out, and the doors are almost always thrown open. Even when the Kona winds kick up, the shaded sidewalk remains cool, and it's especially pleasant at night. Though surrounded by a shopping center, the setting here is anything but mundane. This is Hawaii, after all, and the lush Manoa Valley, backed by the misty Koolau, is more than enough to have you drawing a sharp breath even if you live here. The help tends to be young and cheerful, many of them affiliated in one way or another with the nearby UH.

Like most coffee outlets these days, Manoa sells all the necessary gear for home brewing—espresso makers, thermoses, bean grinders, French-press apparati—as well as an array of bulk coffees, including the local claim to fame, Kona. As is the style in such establishments, the menu is somewhat overwritten. They make one of the better lattes here ($2), nice and hot, though like everyone else they seem to make no practical distinction between that and a cappuccino, so purists may bum slightly. All the usual variations are available—decaf, lowfat milk, mocha, double shot, iced. As Woody Allen once said, they got a language all their own, these guys. Also available are fresh carrot juice, sarsaparilla and lemonade; various teas, herbal and otherwise; Italian sodas made with flavored syrups; and a bracing homemade elixir called Hawaiian Ginger. The small selection of baked goods are made locally and include several types of muffins (raisin walnut—try them with lilikoi butter) and Double Chocolate Macadamia Nut Cake, mahogany-like in both color and density. Delicious, though not the sort of thing you want to bolt just before bodysurfing. Background tunes run in a classical guitar, Windham Hill vein. Live music every Tuesday night, with widely varying results. ♠

Coffee is perhaps more nutritious and certainly more permanent in its stimulating effects, than tea. But its influences, on the whole, are less genial. Taken in large quantities, at once, it not only produces morbid vigilance, but affects the brain, so as to occasion vertigo, and a sort of altered consciousness, or confusion of ideas, not amounting to delirium; which I can compare to nothing so well as the feeling when one is lost amid familiar objects, which look strange, and seem to have their positions, in reference to the points of the compass, changed.

Daniel Drake, M.D., Principal
Diseases of the Interior Valley of
North America (1850)

COFFEE TALK

1152 Koko Head Avenue   KAIMUKI
737-7444   6am-10pm Mon-Th
                                            6am-12am Fri
                                            7am-12am Sat
                                            7am-5pm Sun
VISA, MC   No Alcohol

Coffeehouse
✧

There is an unwritten tenet in the coffeehouse world that says she who displays the most wood, wins. No problem there, and

35

Coffee Talk features more lumber than an episode of *This Old House*. It's an appealingly casual place to meet a friend, read (or write) a novel, or just balance your checkbook. The point is—and I think this is, aside from quality java, the best feature of coffeehouses—you can relax in a pleasant environment, even for several hours if you choose, and nobody pesters you or even particularly notices.

Anyhow, there's usually some nice jazz lilting in the background, and the walls are adorned with works by local artists. As with most nouveau coffee places, the crowd here is Birkenstock-inclined. They show up for the coffee perhaps more than the baked goods or the sandwiches, which are topped by others in the neighborhood (if you're after a truly fine sandwich, whip around the corner to Saigon's). And the java is always good, served hot or cold—denoted on the menu as Heaters and Coolers. House blends and flavored coffees are only a buck a cup, with refills for four bits. They're big into the toddy here—not the David Niven sort, but rather a coffee concentrate made by letting coarsely ground beans soak in water overnight. It's then mixed with more water and the result is quite strong without all the acids that brewing brings out, though it also has a less full-bodied flavor, akin to what you get with a filter drip system. And definitely worth a try is the Coffee Talk milkshake ($3.50), made from espresso, chocolate, vanilla ice cream and bananas—splendid, and rich as the dickens. ♠

Boys should abstain from all use of wine until their eighteenth year, for it is wrong to add fire to fire.
Plato

COLUMBIA INN

645 Kapiolani Boulevard   KAKAAKO
531-3747

3221 Waialae Avenue   KAIMUKI
732-3663
6am-11pm Sun-Th   6am-12am Fri-Sat
VISA, MC, AMEX   Alcohol Served

Coffee Shop
✧

   In a restaurant market as keenly competitive as Hawaii's, eateries seemingly come and go with the trade winds. Having been in
business now for over half a century, the Columbia Inn thus be-
longs to a very select group of establishments which predate not
only statehood, but the Japanese air raid on Pearl Harbor as well.
   Though they've made a few concessions to modern dining trends
(garden burgers, taco salads), this place remains very much a product of its time. What they concentrate on, and definitely what they
do best, is basically the same sturdy fare one finds at full-on Mainland coffee shops and diners. This is comfort food—ribeye steaks,
turkey and dressing, grilled liver and onions. And yet, it bears the
unmistakable markings of the Islands. In fact, a couple of the house
specialties, oxtail soup and saimin, are virtually unavailable in the
contiguous 48. The saimin, by the way, is one of the most expensive
bowls in the state ($6.95) and it comes in what amounts to a small
hot tub loaded with char siu, greens, fish cake, eggs and more.
Generally speaking, entrees run in the $6.50-$10 range.
   Big breakfasts are also happening here, and it's a great place to
stop if you're up early. Waitresses are the professional types, virtually all at least middle-aged and unflappable, clad in crisp uniforms. They keep coffee cups full and dole out big omelets, pancakes, and French toast made with Columbia's homemade breads.
The $5.95 Coach's Platter is particularly popular, and it features
two eggs actually cooked the way you order them, a choice of meats
(the links are particularly good), rice or hash browns, French toast
or pancakes, and fresh fruit. In true coffee shop form there's a large
rotating display, brightly lit and full of pies and chilled papaya
halves. The walls are covered with pictures from the restaurant's
past, autographed shots of celebrities and near-celebrities, and news-
papers describing events of import to the Islands (the Kapiolani
location sits adjacent to Honolulu's two major dailies). ♠

He ordered as one to the menu born.
O. Henry

37

CONTEMPORARY MUSEUM CAFE

2411 Makiki Heights Drive   MAKIKI HEIGHTS
523-3362   11am-2pm Mon-Sat
      (desserts until 3pm)
VISA, MC   Bring Your Own

California Cuisine

✧

It's no secret that hunting for true dining bargains at an art museum is basically an exercise in futility. While the quality of the chow is sometimes quite high, you must be willing to suffer both nouveau-sized portions and some definite gouging on price. This is the case at the (oh so) Contemporary Museum, nestled high up Tantalus in what is otherwise a residential neighborhood. Here the food is tasty, the grounds and the view spectacular, and the pretentiousness sometimes thick enough to cut—beg pardon, *sculpt*— with a chainsaw.

A trip through the museum, which was originally built as a home by the Cooke family in the early part of this century and opened as TCM in 1988, will run you $4. You may want to save it for your meal and instead stroll the grounds for no charge, especially since some of the most interesting artworks are on the back lawn, anyway. And besides, you won't want to miss the impressive gardens, which were originally constructed between 1928 and 1949 and have about them a pleasing look of permanence. Rock walkways, high hedges, enormous eucalyptus trees, Honolulu and the Pacific as a backdrop— you've got to love it.

Around to the right you'll find the cafe, with seating outside on the lanai as well as a nice indoor dining room with a cool stone floor and plenty of art on display. The menu has a sort of Wolfgang Puckish ring to it, and offerings include Malaysian shrimp salad topped with a light peanut sauce, smoked mahi salad with a delicious lingonberry vinaigrette, and a pretty fair Caesar. From the sandwich board both the grilled eggplant and the tempeh (nice and firm, well-cooked, topped with tahini dressing) are pretty splendid, sided by olives, peppers, and a scant spoonful of tabouli. Iced coffee and iced tea seem to be the beverages of choice. A sniffy hostess may ask if you have reservations even if half the tables are empty, and the waiters tend to be husky, slightly brooding young guys in shorts and hightops. TCM members and their guests get 20% off their food bill, so make friends. ♠

When ordering lunch, the big executives are just as indecisive as the rest of us.
William Feather

COUSIN'S

2970 E. Manoa Road   MANOA
988-5592
565 Paiea Street (lunch wagon)   KALIHI
833-4402
9:30am-2pm Mon-Fri   10am-2pm Sat
No Plastic   No Alcohol

Plate Lunch

At a time when plate lunch seems to have pretty well gone to hell in a handbasket, Cousin's does more than it's share to foster respectability in the discipline. Quite likely the smallest restaurant in existence with double doors, it's interior is simple in the extreme: a cafeteria-type contraption housing steam trays and doubling as a counter, chilled items dispensed from an Igloo cooler, a filing cabinet and mammoth ice machine lending further ambience. The floor is postmodernist concrete, with space for perhaps four svelte adults to wait in Tokyo subway-style coziness. Needless to report, everything is for takeout.

The kitchen is correspondingly diminutive but this enterprising gang accomplishes plenty with what they've got, cranking out consistently fine meals for bottom dollar (most run about $4). True to the plate lunch creed, Cousin's menu is a straightforward index of favorites: grilled mahi, shoyu chicken, sweet-and-sour spareribs, a truly awesome chicken cutlet. The curry beef stew is a mouth-watering amalgam of lean beef, carrots, and potatoes in a golden gravy, tinged with coriander and cumin. The daily special to watch for is grilled ahi, and everything is served with mac salad and two scoops rice as required by state law. Pickled Maui onions add a much needed dimension, the puckery bite a perfect foil for meats and neutral starches. Though minor, an inspired touch.

39

On Aloha Fridays they serve up a modified Hawaiian Plate ($5.25) featuring one of if not the best lau lau on Oahu. Purists may decry it as unauthentic for lack of fish, but that's failing to see the big picture. Cousin's starts with a lean and large hunk of juicy pork wrapped in fresh taro leaf, then subjects it to a steaming unparalleled in Western annals since Jimmy Swaggart quit wearing his glasses to the topless donut shop. Simply terrific. The food often runs out by midafternoon and closing time is therefore a rather elastic concept, so call first to see what's up. ♠

Economy is the art of making the most of life. The love of economy is the root of all virtue.
George Bernard Shaw

CRACK SEED STORE

1156 Koko Head Avenue

737-1022

No Plastic

KAIMUKI

9am-6pm Mon-Sat

10:30am-4:30pm Sun

No Alcohol

Crack Seed

✧

Initially of Chinese origin, the array of preserved fruits and seeds collectively known as crack seed is now a thoroughly Hawaiian phenomenon. However, like shave ice, lau lau, and numerous other items integral to the Island gastronomic identity, it has grown increasingly difficult to find in its natural habitat, i.e., the neighborhood store.

Crack Seed Store is one of a dwindling number of shops that survive despite the skyrocketing cost of living and doing business in Hawaii. It has presumably benefited from relatively low overhead—the entire store is perhaps 10 feet by 12 feet—and its location in one of Oahu's more vibrant neighborhoods. The proprietor is a small, demure gentleman who can usually be seen bobbing amid the sea of glass jars, filling bags with quality goods like wasabi peas, sweet-and-sour papaya, pumpkin seeds, dried cranberries, preserved guava peel, sweet-salty mango, various types of lemon peel (very sour), and on and on. The arare (mochi crunch) is an excellent bargain, with a 1-pound bag going for about $5; it's good enough to make you laugh out loud the next time someone makes a loving reference to Chex mix. A sort of house specialty, if you will, is arare

40

doused with a ladleful of the racy liquid from the jar of wet li hing mui. The owner is understandably proud of this creation, but it must be eaten immediately or it quickly becomes reminiscent of something you might encounter on a moviehouse floor. ♠

The man who hoards his ginger and nibbles his salt is a true miser.

Chinese proverb

CREPE FEVER/MOCHA JAVA

1200 Ala Moana Boulevard   ALA MOANA
521-9023/537-3611   8am-9pm Mon-Sat
                                             8am-4pm Sun
VISA, MC   Alcohol Served

Breakfast/Coffee
✧

The Ward Centre is pretty much of a wasteland for food, cheap or otherwise, and anathema for bargain hunters in general. Most of the shops are devoted to designer clothing, jewelry, crystal, and the like; full-on retail's the law of the land here. In the midst of this scene—frequented during the day by ridiculously overdressed women of means, Japanese flight attendants, and the occasional elderly tourists in knee socks who seem to have lost their way—Crepe Fever serves up good food at only slightly inflated prices.

For no apparent reason, this is actually one restaurant posing as two (despite appearances, you can order at either counter and sit wherever you like). Breakfast is a big production, and served all the time. The breakfast chapati ($6 or so) features veggies and eggs, and it's tasty; ditto the fritatta. Best picks on the crepes are either the boneless, skinless Mexican chicken or the lemon spinach—if you can't decide, try both for about $8. Should you fancy your crepes in more of a dessert configuration, try the bananas and cream. Tuna sandwiches are made with water-packed albacore, shredded cheddar, and plenty of hard-boiled eggs. Homemade soups vary and are

41

usually a strong suit. Since Ward Centre tends to attract women bent on light-eating, portions here can hardly be described as enormous.

Mocha Java offers coffees of the day for around a buck a cup, plus lattes, a very intense espresso milkshake, and something called a Mocha Chocolattayaya ($3.95)—espresso, chocolate, ice cream, and a liberal glob of Jif peanut butter. This bad boy is as rich as they come, and will either have you barreling toward nirvana or hurling on the sidewalk, depending on your threshold for such things. Use your best judgement. ♠

Cheese—milk's leap forward to immortality.
Clifton Fadiman, Any Number Can
Play (1957)

DAI RYU HOUSE OF NOODLES

1610 S. King Street   PAWAA
941-1939   11am-10pm Mon-Sat
No Plastic   Bring Your Own

Japanese Noodles
✧

You've got to love open-kitchen restaurants—the smells, the action, the billows of steam. Dai Ryu is performance art as it ought to be, and such is the petiteness of the place that you can very to be, and such is the petite-   ness of the place
that you can very   nearly reach over
and give the wok a   shake   yourself,
though this might   draw frowns from the
staff. The menu is   noodles and nothing
but: choose from either   rahmen (soup noodles in
an excellent miso broth) or   yakisoba (fried noodles), and
give strongest consideration to   either the mabo tofu or
gomoku versions. A couple   of cold noodle dishes are
also offered. The staff   banters back and forth
in Japanese, and all   dishes are cooked
when ordered so   they come too you
plenty hot. The   downside to this,
since there are only two woks going, is that your dining companion may be halfway through his meal by the time yours arrives. But hey, it's service with a smile and the prices are very reasonable,

virtually everything falling in the $5-$6 range. And did I mention that the portions are quite generous? ♠

To eat is human, to digest, divine.
Anonymous

D'AMICOS HONEST PIZZA

59-026 Kam Highway	HALEIWA/NORTH SHORE
638-9611	7am-9pm Daily
No Plastic	Alcohol Served

Pizza
✧

On an island where great pizza is all but nonexistent, this place, the last outpost along the great surfing beaches of the North Shore, stands as a man among boys. There are two types of pies, either whisper-thin New York-style or the thicker Deluxe version. The New York is quite distinctive, with a crust that's incredibly thin yet still possessing a remarkable degree of integrity, never veering into sogginess. It's spread with a scant layer of tomato sauce and a blend of cheeses. Available whole ($12.95 for a plain 16-inch) or by the slice ($1.95), toppings include fresh mushrooms and superb Italian sausage, crumbled and not oily in the least. The thicker pizzas ($17-$18 for a 16-inch) come in three varieties—vegetarian, Eddie's (tomatoes, sausage, pepperoni, fresh garlic, mushrooms, black olives), and the sans-tomato White Pie, made with ricotta, fresh garlic, garlic butter, onion, and mushrooms.

Other items of note are the Italian salad and the mahi sub, served on sturdy Italian bread. The massive lasagna is also widely admired—it's made with spinach, ricotta, mozzarella, provolone, parmesan and Kitty's secret gravy, all spilling out of an undersized vessel ($6.95). The interior is pleasant enough, with bamboo, a black and white tile floor, and the obligatory surf paraphernalia, including a poster for the Quiksilver—an event held only when the waves are 20 feet or larger, in memory of local legend and big-wave master Eddie Aikau who disappeared at sea in 1978. As is frequently the case on the North Shore, the waitresses have a penchant for halter tops. Weekends are busy, but keep an eye out for one of the lanai tables. Dessert is cheesecake, or check out the macadamia cream pies next door at Ted's Bakery. ♠

43

If a man will be sensible and one fine morning, while he is lying in bed, count at the tips of his fingers how many things in this life truly give him pleasure, invariably he will find food is the first one.

Lin Yutang

DA SMOKEHOUSE

470 Ena Road   WAIKIKI

946-0233   11am-12am Daily

No Plastic   Bring Your Own

Barbecue

✧

As with most things culinary, the term barbecue has connotations in Hawaii quite apart from those on the Mainland. You see it advertised all over town, but this invariably means Asian barbecue, most often Korean or Chinese. Though often phenomenal in their own right, these bear little resemblance to the slow-smoked meats one finds in Texas (beef) and the South (pork). Ironically, probably the closest thing you'll find to these in the Islands is kalua pig, a luau staple that's slow-cooked in an imu but never referred to as barbecue and rarely eaten in sandwich form. Confused?

Anyhow, Da Smokehouse is one of the few places in Hawaii you'll find Mainland-inspired barbecue. It's Texas-style, more or less; besides some pretty fair beef ribs and grilled chicken that's merely average, they serve up a mean beef brisket sandwich. The meat's chopped in sizable hunks—not sliced, not stringy, insanely tender—and piled on a sesame bun. Unless you say otherwise, it's doused with a dark, tomato-based sauce that's somewhat sweet and extremely tangy, with faint but cumulative heat. This is a messy, splendid, substantial thing, as it should be for $5.50.

Side orders—you get two with full dinners—include baked beans, corn on the cob, and homemade French fries which, though touted, are too chunky and uncrisp to excite. The cole slaw, on the other hand, is excellent. As basic as you'll find, it consists only of crunchy green cabbage shaved thin and dressed with a sweet and tangy mayo/vinegar concoction—same as you'd find in a Mississippi catfish joint. Most of the business here is takeout and they do deliver, but you seem to make out a little better portionwise if you eat here. Dinners are in the $5-$10 range.

Counting the ones out front there are about 10 tables. The decor is a combination of wood and brick, much of it bearing the auto-graphs of satisfied patrons. Doors and windows are always open so it's not too smoky even with the action in the kitchen. They'll also custom smoke anything you've got, within reason. ♠

Everything which inflames one appetite is likely to arouse the others also...and even salt, in any but the smallest quantity, is objectionable; it is such a goad toward carnalism that the ancient fable depicted Ve-nus as born of the salt sea wave.

Dio Lewis, A.M., M.D., Chastity: or,
Our Secret Sins (1874)

DAVE'S ICE CREAM

85-786 Farrington Highway	WAIANAE
696-9294	
41-1537 Kalanianaole Highway	WAIMANALO
259-8576	
819 Kapahulu Avenue	KAPAHULU
735-2194	
98-820 Moanalua Road	AIEA
487-7887	
Sears	ALA MOANA CENTER
944-9663	
94-1040 Waipio Uka	WAIPAHU
677-0028	
94-050 Farrington Highway	WAIPAHU
677-5016	
Pearl Kai Food Court	PEARL CITY
487-3053	
98-199 Kam Highway	AIEA
487-3053	
11am-10pm Mon-Th	11am-11pm Fri-Sun
	(call—hours vary by location)
No Plastic	No Alcohol

Ice Cream
✧

Dave's cranks out what many Hawaii residents consider the best ice cream in the state, and ardent admirers tout several of their flavors as being among the finest anywhere. At any rate, Dave's boasts one of the more eclectic flavor lists around, and they make extensive use of local ingredients. Their smooth and fragrant sherbets are made with fresh lychee, guava, mango and passion fruit; the ice creams (especially rich thanks to a high butterfat content) contain Kona coffee, coconut, macadamia nuts and poha berries, which have a pleasant sourness reminiscent of gooseberries.

The most intriguing item on the premises is the green tea ice cream, which also happens to be their top seller. More dense than some of the fruit flavors, the taste is complex, distinctive, exquisite. Not too sweet, it's unlikely to put you in mind of the organic, leafiness of green tea (or any other kind of tea, for that matter), and it has an almost chocolatey quality about it—fact is, it probably won't remind you of anything else you've had. But it's as good as ice cream gets, so don't miss out. Two scoops on a cone will run you $2.50, and they also have shakes, splits, and the like. ♠

You can taste and feel, but not describe, the exquisite state of repose produced by tea, that precious drink which drives away the five causes of sorrow.
Emperor Chien Lung (1710-1799), Manchu Dynasty

DETROIT ITALIAN DELI

121 Hekili Street   KAILUA
262-DELI (3354)   10am-7pm Mon-Fri
                                                        11am-4pm Sat
No Plastic   Bring Your Own

Sandwiches
✧

Proprietor Kevin Braekevelt, a former boxer, has turned his Italian-style deli into something of shrine to Detroit-area sports teams. What with all the pictures of Norm Cash, Bill Freehan and Tiger Stadium, not to mention the mug shots of gap-toothed greats from the Red Wings' days of yore, one can't help but be impressed by his allegiance.

Even more moving than a man who still has positive words to say about Denny McLain are the sandwiches he builds—hefty, hearty subs that rank with any you'll find in Hawaii. You won't go far wrong with any of the 15 or so sandwiches offered here, and figure on anything with salami being especially choice. That includes both the Detroit and Sicilian subs, which come sprinkled with Italian dressing and pepperoncini. The cold sandwiches can get a bit messy, but the wonderfully chewy bread is capable of absorbing healthy doses of olive oil, vinegar, and sundry other condiments without turning to mush. Best call on the hot sandwiches is the Italian sausage, lean and full of spice. Subs run about $4-$4.50 for a 6-incher, $7-$8 for a footlong. They also serve smooth and distinctive Vernor's Ginger Ale, which is to Detroit Italian delis what Dr. Brown's sodas are to New York Jewish ones. ♠

Do not talk while eating, lest the windpipe act before the gullet, and life be endangered.
Johanan, Talmud: Taanit

DEW DROP INN

1088 S. Beretania Street	MAKIKI
526-9522	10:30am-2pm, 5pm-9pm Tue-Sat
	5pm-9pm Sun
VISA, MC	Bring Your Own

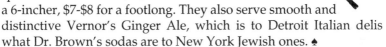

Northern Chinese

✧

There's probably at least one Dew Drop Inn in every city and town in America. Usually they're either roadhouses where Harley riders gather amid roars and clanking bottles, or the sort of juke joints Otis Redding might have played during his chitlin-circuit days. But it seems safe to venture that nowhere else in the land, in fiction or reality, is there a Dew Drop Inn specializing in Northern Chinese food. Only in Makiki.

There are but seven tables here, accented by pink cloths, plastic plants, and swag lamps. A steady stream of 70's light rock converges midair with kitchen banter, the clatter of pots and silverware, and the low hum of the A/C. Lunch specials are an excellent deal: $4 gets you set up with items like kung pao shrimp (properly fiery with plenty of red chiles and water chestnuts), crispy-fried chicken, and a fine mabo tofu. Lunches portions are fairly modest, so give some thought to the hot and sour soup ($1.25/cup). Or if you're dining with a friend, jump on the chicken and chive pot stickers. Service is very accommodating and the command of English here is well above the norm, so avoiding things like MSG or animal products shouldn't be a problem.

At dinner the menu expands to include recommended items like the house special sizzling garlic shrimp, jung bao chicken with vegetables in sweet bean sauce, and a real proper mu shiu pork with vegetables, eggs, and the requisite Mandarin pancakes and plum sauce. With the exception of a few seafood dishes, $5-$6 buys anything you see. ♠

The jukebox was giving out with a stomp version of "Big-Legged Woman." Saxaphones were pleading; the horns were teasing; the bass was patting; the drums were chatting; the piano was catting, laying and playing the jive, and a husky female voice was shouting: "...You can feel my thigh. But don't you feel up high."

Chester Himes (description of events at the Dew Drop Inn), The Real Cool Killers (1959)

DIEM

2633 S. King Street
941-8657/943-8657
VISA, MC

MOILIILI
10am-10pm Daily
Bring Your Own

Vietnamese

The French colonial experience in Vietnam was disastrous with a capital D, what with the humidity and the locals gagging on a steady diet of exploitation and Maurice Chevalier records. Foodwise, though, we can at least be thankful that the British weren't involved, as the lasting influence the French exerted on the native cuisine comes far nearer to an East-meets-West success story. Vietnamese iced coffee is a simple but compelling illustration of this, but the Continental sway is in evidence at Diem far beyond the potable realm. Dishes of interest include chicken with crabmeat stuffing (about $7) and the throw rug-sized shrimp crepe ($6), which arrives piping hot and drooping off the ends of the plate. Eggier and larger than French crepes, it's meant to be wrapped in lettuce and dipped in a sweet vinegar sauce—scrumptious, though eerily suggestive of something Wilma Flintstone might've whipped up after a jaunt to the pterodactyl's nest.

Among the appetizers, the beef wrapped in spicy herbs ($4 range) is a model of gastronomic foreplay, shamelessly arousing the palate without dulling the appetite. Spring rolls are superb and

available as an entree, accompanied by
fresh lettuce, cold vermicelli,
and mint leaves— wrap these
together and have at it. Barbecue chicken w i t h
golden rice is another
w i n n e r — boneless
and juicy, t o p p e d
with fresh coconut.
The din- ing area is
cozy and pleasant, over-
seen by a gentle- man so soft-spoken
he makes Mother Theresa seem like a cir-
cus barker. The proprietors appear to be
firmly in the throes of their Blue Period—
blue walls, blue trim, blue curtains—and surprisingly inter- esting framed displays trace
the evolution of Vietnamese currency, complete
with samples. Extensive use is made of those
friends to White House economists and small-
restaurant own- ers alike—mirrors. Also offered
is a decent shabu shabu, though it's recommended only for light eaters. They pour a nice
cup of mellow jasmine tea, and there's tapioca with coconut milk for dessert. Carpe Diem. ♠

They sat at a corner table in the little restaurant, eating with gusto and noise after the manner of simple-hearted people who like their neighbors to see and know their pleasures.

Jean Rhys, The Left Bank (1927)

DINKI DINKY

100 N. Beretania Street   CHINATOWN
No Phone   10am-6pm Mon-Fri
                                     10am-3pm Sat
No Plastic   No Alcohol

Chinese Ice Cake

✧

    This store is so tiny it holds at maximum two adults, and for the most part they traffic in candy, sodas, pogs, and other knickknacks of little interest to the serious eater. However, Dinki's warrants mention in these pages because they also peddle a Chinese treat known as ice cake. It's really nothing more than juice and a few bits of fruit frozen in a plastic cup, but what makes it interesting—and an excellent follow-up to a serious Chinatown feed—are the flavors: lychee (spelled here as "lai chee"), azuki bean, coconut, li hing mui, guava, pineapple, even starfruit, though they frequently run out of this. Prices are around 75 cents, and they come with a small wooden spoon that remains nigh on useless until things melt a bit.

    Just outside is a cluster of tables where spirited games of mahjongg and cards attract throngs of elderly folks from the neighborhood—as well as the occasional befuddled derelict. Posted in the window is a hand-lettered sign sternly announcing, "We Reserve the Right of Refusal for Any Purchasement." With minimal prompting the owners will cajole their oversized, emerald-green parakeet, Lulu, into ringing her little bell for customers. ♠

Sweet melon lips, bitter melon heart.
Chinese proverb

DOONG KONG LAU—HAKKA CUISINE

100 N. Beretania Street   CHINATOWN
531-8833/521-8848   9am-9:30pm Mon-Fri
                               8am-9:30pm Sat-Sun
VISA, MC   Alcohol Served

Chinese Hakka Cuisine

✧

    In a sea of Chinese restaurants, this is the only one offering what's known as Hakka cuisine. Driven from their home in the

Northern mountains centuries ago, the Hakkas migrated south, bringing along their distinctive cooking style. The menu here is especially diverse, divided into no less that 21 subcategories. There's a pronounced emphasis on seafood—scallops are available eight different ways and squid six, including in an excellent hot garlic sauce ($5.95). You'll do well ordering a mound of noodles, as well as any of the casseroles—savory, bubbling affairs cooked and served in heavy metal crocks. Plenty of choices ($7-$8), including chicken with black mushroom and roasted fish with scallion.

For some reason virtually every Chinese restaurant on Oahu lists eggplant in hot garlic sauce as a house specialty, and Doong Kong Lau is no exception. The cook also rightly recommends the Sauteed Stuffed Tofu Hakka-Style, which is filled with pork hash and fish cake; it can also be had deep-fried in a sizzling platter format. And speaking of sizzling platters, the $7.95 seafood combination is as tasty as it is noisy, hopping with shrimp, scallops, and assorted vegetables. If waterfowl are a turn-on, check out the deep-fried duck with lemon sauce. Though this is definitely quality bird, it's the sauce that makes it—golden and slightly sweet, with flavor to burn thanks to a perfect melding of two of the planet's finer entities, lemon and ginger. It's served on the side to facilitate deep dunking and direct bodily application.

Doong Kong Lau's interior is spacious, and, shall we say color-ful: carpet so short and so green that you may experience involuntary pangs of remorse at having left your putter at home, nicely complemented by peach tablecloths that very nearly match the carp drifting aimlessly in the tanks by the door. Shabu shabu is offered at night. These folks also own a place in North Seattle. ♠

In a Chinese restaurant you should order one dish for each person present, although no hard and fast rule can be made because of the varying size of the dishes. For four people you might, for example, order a soup, a seafood dish, a chicken dish, a pork dish, and perhaps an egg dish or beef with vegetables. The purpose is variety not only in taste but also in texture.
Calvin Lee, Chinatown, USA (1965)

DOWN TO EARTH DELI

2525 S. King Street   MOILIILI
947-7678   10am-9pm Daily
VISA, MC   No Alcohol

Vegetarian
✧

Since changing hands a while back, the menu here has taken a more international turn. Located in a corner of Honolulu's finest grocery, it's a favorite haunt of UH students, vegetarians, and spirulina-happy New Agers. And its definitely the chow that's the draw, as atmosphere is negligible—a few counter stools, a small eating area upstairs, and the constant beeping of cash registers for background noise.

Essentially what you have here is a miniature cafeteria line. The salad bar, though small, is very nice—after all, where can fresh vegetables be had if not in a grocery store?—and features some fine homemade dressings, green goddess and creamy italian among them. Price is by the pound. They offer a few sandwiches as well as tempeh burgers, but these are pre-made; skip them in favor of hot items ($3-$5) like coconut curry and vegetables, Mexican casserole, or minestrone. The vegetarian chili is also happening, served over brown rice. Though everything's made here, you'll have better luck with Asian-influenced dishes than, say, Italian ones (sorry, but you just can't make a real calzone with butter). East or West, the tendency is to go easy on the spices, particularly pepper of all shades.

Other savory items include Indian samosas and bhondas (potatoes and chickpea flour rolled into balls and fried) with chutney, and a variety of prepared salads. The best of these are the Pasta Veggie, made with cockle shells, red and gold peppers and the aforementioned Italian dressing, and the tabouli, laced with minced veggies—non-traditional, but very tasty. Items such as potato salad and cole slaw are made with soy mayonnaise. The baked goods selection is ever-changing, but it features the likes of blueberry coffeecake, carob cake, and a nice apple crumb. Muffins, good but a shade dry, include pumpkin, banana, blueberry, and raisin bran. Among the fresh juice possibilities are wheat grass at $2 a shot and a spinach/celery/carrot combo, in case you're interested. ♠

He that takes medicine and neglects diet, wastes the skill of the physician.
Chinese proverb

EASTERN PARADISE

1403 S. King Street
941-5858
VISA, MC

PAWAA
10am-9:30pm Tue-Sun
Alcohol Served

Northern Chinese

✧

I've yet to discover why a restaurant specializing in Northern Chinese cuisine calls itself Eastern Paradise. And while we're on the subject of confusing monikers, take note that the Szechuan province is technically in Western China, but it's commonly accepted practice in the restaurant business to use the terms Szechuan and Northern Chinese interchangeably. Whatever the case, they both translate to mean spicy—sometimes very spicy. The soups here are excellent, and the hot and sour ranks alongside the best around. It's rich and complex, with a nice bite that never crosses the boundary into scorching. Unlike many lesser versions, it's loaded with all manner of goodies: pork, tofu, black mushrooms, vegetables, even abalone.

All meals include hot tea and fairly racy (and unlimited) kim chee, rare in a Chinese eatery. It's tasty but an insidious appetite-killer, so go easy. You'll want to be fully operational when it comes time to tackle dishes like the spicy fried squid, its sauce laden with red chile flakes and magnificent in both the tangy and hot sense.

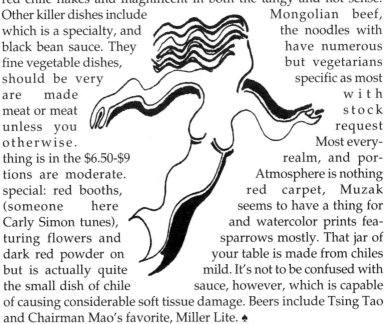

Other killer dishes include which is a specialty, and black bean sauce. They fine vegetable dishes, should be very are made meat or meat unless you otherwise. thing is in the $6.50-$9 tions are moderate. special: red booths, (someone here Carly Simon tunes), turing flowers and dark red powder on but is actually quite the small dish of chile Mongolian beef, the noodles with have numerous but vegetarians specific as most with stock request Most every- realm, and por- Atmosphere is nothing red carpet, Muzak seems to have a thing for and watercolor prints fea- sparrows mostly. That jar of your table is made from chiles mild. It's not to be confused with sauce, however, which is capable of causing considerable soft tissue damage. Beers include Tsing Tao and Chairman Mao's favorite, Miller Lite. ♠

53

> *...We hadn't been south of Thirty-fifth Street, east of Fifth Avenue or north of Fifty-ninth. But we'd been thorough. We'd had pizza, coconut juice, pastrami, pig's feet, paella, and Him Soon York, and Lamaar had been sick on the corner of Broadway and Forty-fourth Street.*
>
> **William Price Fox**, "Hello New York" (1968)

EGGS 'N THINGS

1911 Kalakaua Avenue WAIKIKI
949-0820 11pm-2pm Daily
No Plastic Bring Your Own

Breakfast

✧

This is perhaps the best known breakfast spot in Waikiki, and one of a very few that has much to say for itself. Such is the reputation that crowds—the overwhelming majority are tourists arriving on foot, mainly because parking around here is an A-1 bitch—routinely gather in the a.m., especially on weekends. Waits are common if not a certainty at these times, but they go pretty quickly. The menu, which comes to you on a cumbersome lacquered board, is extensive and augmented by a number of specials scrawled in a barely legible hand on the back wall. Fresh swordfish and eggs is a must if offered; otherwise, there's some type of fresh fish virtually every day, caught by the restaurant's owner on his early morning boat runs.

Other dishes include burly three-egg omelettes ($7-$8), though these are often somewhat dull. Everything's served with a side of three extraordinary pancakes—light, fluffy, slightly springy, able to withstand a dousing of syrup without turning to wet Kleenex. Speaking of syrups, the boysenberry is excellent, as is the coconut cream. The tangy fruit sauce is better still, kind of like pourable orange marmalade.

Besides the flapjacks, waffles and French toast are the other strong suits. Keep an eye peeled for a particularly compelling version of the latter made with fresh papaya, macadamia nuts and whipped cream—every Hawaiian breakfast should be this good. Whatever you order you'll pay a bit much, this being Waikiki, but tapeworm-free patrons will definitely not leave hungry. Hours here are quite unusual, and like just about everyone else in Waikiki with a stove, they offer an early riser's special: between 5 and 9 a.m. and 1 to 2 p.m., you can get two eggs and three pancakes for $2.75. Such a deal.

Decor is pretty standard coffee shop stuff, with plenty of synthetic verdure, including the banana tree in the corner; skillets and pans pertinent to the trade; some framed pictures of Waikiki in pre-statehood days; and a sign featuring the heads of a pig, chicken, and cow with the words "Please Eat Fish." One wall is covered with shellacked covers of old Hawaiian sheet music. Waitresses are the career types and very competent despite the crowds. While you're in the neighborhood, check out The Military Store a few doors down. Here you'll find all sorts of necessities, from MRE's to snazzy German marching boots to the latest issue of *Soldier of Fortune*. ♠

If I were given my choice between an egg and ambrosia for breakfast, I should choose an egg.
Robert Lynd

EJ'S PIZZA

85-773 Farrington Highway   WAIANAE
696-9676   10:30am-9pm Daily
No Plastic   No Alcohol

Pizza/Sandwiches/Mexican

EJ's apparent (albeit unstated) philosophy is this: You can, in fact, please all of the people all of the time. To be sure the jack-of-all-trades idea plays better out this way since there are relatively few restaurants, and the menu features everything from burritos to pizza (which they do reasonably well), tacos to sandwiches, salads to barbecue beef and chicken with a choice of side orders (beans, corn on the cob, cole slaw). Though none of the grinds are of genius quality, virtually everything is satisfactory, and prices are quite reasonable—a five spot buys just about anything. There's no indoor seating, so either take it with you—perhaps to Pokai Bay or any of the beaches along here, which remain Oahu's best-kept secret—or hunker down at one of the outdoor tables, though these are a bit close to the highway traffic. They don't have parking, so you have to do your best to snake a spot in one of the neighboring lots. ♠

A smiling face is half the meal.
Latvian proverb

EL BURRITO

550 Piikoi Street

533-3457

No Plastic

ALA MOANA

11am-8pm Mon-Th

11am-9pm Fri-Sat

Bring Your Own

Mexican

✧

El Burrito is across the street from Ala Moana Center, in a small building that also houses a couple of modest pawn shops—kind of handy should you need to hock your watch for meal money. The interior is small (10 tables), clean, and quite attractive, with textured taupe walls and hardwood flooring; the muted turquoise-and-maroon color scheme exudes a decidedly un-Pacific ambience.

Much of the menu consists of a la carte items like burritos, chimichangas, tostadas, enchiladas, chile relleno and tacos made with soft corn tortillas. They also serve menudo and a pretty fair lamb consomme. When ordering, try to keep in mind that these folks seem to understand meats better than they do vegetables. Tacos run in the $3 range, tostadas closer to $4, and burritos about $5. For an extra $1.50 or so you can get full plates with rice and beans; unfortunately, there are no combination plates. The fresh salsa is an uncooked, tomatoey version with modest fire.

Best bet is the tacos, which are served with a refreshing and nearly heatless pico de gallo. For fillings, try either the steak or the tender hunks of roasted lamb, which smells more muttony than it tastes. The chimichangas are a strong choice as well, but the burritos are only average, suffering as much as anything from FTS (Fragile Tortilla Syndrome). The music here is usually pleasant, selected from a large cache of tapes that cover the

Latin spectrum from Ruben Blades to mariachi standards. Flan is the lone dessert offering. ♠

Part of the secret of success in life is to eat what you like and let the food fight it out inside.
Mark Twain

EL CHARRO AVITIA

14 Oneawa Street   KAILUA
263-3943   11am-9pm Daily
VISA, MC   Alcohol Served

Mexican
✧

Given the breadth of their menu, the consistently high caliber of their ingredients, and their beguiling way with seafood, a strong argument can be advanced that this is the best Mexican restaurant on the island. Though they've only been in business in Hawaii for a brief time, the Avitia family opened their first restaurant in Bishop, California almost two decades ago. Since that time, Dona Inez Avitia and her crew have opened others in Nevada and California; now, to our considerable benefit, her youngest son Tony and wife Tina have set up shop in Kailua town.

What you'll find here is an authenticity sorely lacking in most local Mexican eateries. It actually looks and feels like a restaurant you might find just off the zocalo in Oaxaca: tile floor, turquoise walls, mariachi tunes, lots of family pictures, and some nifty pre-Columbian style artworks. All the basics—chips and salsa, beans, tortillas—are solid, and rice is available in Spanish and white lime versions. Besides the usual combination plates of tacos, enchiladas, chile relleno and burritos, they offer interesting specialties like fresh, limey ceviche tacos. The Tacos Nacionales is two soft tortillas wrapped around chicken, cream cheese and almonds, garnished with a Mexican flag. Robust appetites will applaud the burrito del rey—a flour tortilla stuffed with chicken, beans, and plenty of mild green chiles, it's big enough to set sail on. Seafood triumphs include the camarones chipotle (made with shrimp and a particularly fierce and flavorful jalapeno that has been dried and smoked) and the fresh opakapaka with papaya-avocado salsa. If you're wanting to go the limit, show up on a Friday or Saturday night when they offer crepas del mar: jumbo shrimp, scallops, and the fresh catch, all

57

sauteed with white wine and mushrooms, swaddled in fresh crepes and topped with white sauce and pomegranate seeds. It's served with black beans and sauteed vegetables, and you'll need a little time to sleep this one off. The one drawback to El Charro Avitia (and most every other Island Mexican eatery), is that the prices can threaten the upper limits for cheap eating. Seafood plates run in the $10-$15 range, with everything else about $7.50-$10. Desserts include flan and a monstrous fried ice cream coated with almonds and cinnamon honey. ♠

The best sauce in the world is hunger.
Miguel de Cervantes, Don Quixote

EL CHOLO

823 California Avenue   WAHIAWA
621-0474   10:30am-9pm Mon-Sat
No Plastic   Bring Your Own

Mexican
✧

Though excellent cheap meals abound in the Isles, good Mexican takeout is an all but nonexistent term in the Hawaii dining lexicon. Either you go for the full sit-down experience at Quintero's or El Charro Avitia, or you throw quality concerns to the breeze and Run for the Border, as it were. El Cholo is the one real alternative to these polar extremes, and it's fittingly located in the GI burg of Wahiawa, a hotbed of excellent non-Asian cheap eats.

Before their recent move to a modern shopping center, El Cholo inhabited California Avenue digs so small and scruffy and hot you had to keep reminding yourself you weren't in San Antonio. But if some of the character has been lost, the grinds are still well worth seeking out. For $2-$3 bucks you can get enchiladas, chile verde, chimichangas. The tacos are filled with either beef or chicken and aren't what they could be, but the burritos are hefty and good, and cheapest on the island by several bucks. The must-try item is the gordita, a small, thick tortilla made fresh, then split and stuffed with meat, beans, and cheese. Though it doesn't equal those you'll find in the border states, it's an anomaly in these parts and tasty, too. ♠

Primitive society tells us where it's at. Our business is basically sex and hunger.
Henry G. Walter, International Flavors and Fragrances

ELENA'S

94-300 Farrington Highway   WAIPAHU
671-3279
2153 N. King Street   KALIHI
845-0340

6am-8:45pm Daily
VISA, MC   No Alcohol

Filipino
✧

Unlike most every other Asian cuisine, Filipino food has never achieved much in the way of crossover success in the States. Though far more prevalent and appreciated in Hawaii than on the Mainland, even here its considerable merits remain relatively unsung. Some cite the Filipino penchant for tripe and organ meats; others blame the strong tendency toward salty and sour flavors (often in combination) as being unsettling to timid American palates. Regardless of what you may have heard, though, Filipino food is quite worth investigating.

Just as Vietnamese cuisine was supplied with a Western influence via the French, so too were Filipino grinds altered by three centuries of Spanish presence. Elena's menu bears witness to this, and items such as pork gisantes—a hearty stew made with tomatoes and green peas—have become standards. While a few of the dishes here are nothing special (skip the adobo, for example), many, like the shrimp sinigang, are excellent, as are side items like the banana lumpia ($2.25). What's more, Elena's offers a number of specials not always found elsewhere, authentic treasures like fried bangus (milkfish), crispy pata, and pig's feet soup, which seems to have a particularly ardent following in the Waipahu community. As is the Filipino custom, everything is served with a monster bowl of rice and most dishes are the same price; the magic number here is $5.85. Breakfast is also offered, and besides the usual Island rendi-

59

tions of eggs, rice and Spam, they offer infinitely more stimulating possibilities: eggs with the spicy sausage known as longaniza ($4.50), a fried rice omelette ($5), and fried rice adobo ($4.50). The atmosphere's nothing special, equal parts fake wood veneer, hand-lettered signs, and bad art, punctuated by feisty discussions, in Tagalog, between the numerous women minding the shop at any given time. ♠

Seeing is deceiving. It's eating that's believing.
James Thurber (1956)

EMILIO'S PIZZA

1423 Kalakaua Avenue   PAWAA
946-4972   5pm-11pm Mon-Th
                                                   5pm-12am Fri-Sat
VISA, MC   Bring Your Own

Italian

✧

In the pizza-impaired city of Honolulu, Emilio's has more than a few staunch supporters who maintain they serve the best pies for several thousand miles in all directions. And on some nights, at least, they do; trouble is, you never know which nights. Because they start from scratch (which is why the wait can be a long one), Emilio's quality varies more than the chain parlors's (which settle for mediocrity, but consistent mediocrity). But other than the occasional off night, these folks do up a nice pie: thick crust, oregano-laced sauce that's more tomatoey than tangy, fresh toppings, and high-grade cheeses. They don't sell slices, and you can expect to shell out around $15 for a 14-inch pie with two toppings, most of which are standards; pineapple and jalapenos provide the lone whiffs of exotica. If you hanker for a tomatoless pie, check out the pizza bianco—that's garlic, garlic butter, basil, mozzarella, ricotta, parmesan, and romano. It's serious stuff, but if your in the mood it's terrific. Otherwise, the sandwiches (around $6) are so-so as is the pasta, but the hefty calzones ($8.50) are something else again, and they come with a house salad. The atmosphere is romantic in a basic sort of way—a handful of tables draped with checked cloths, candles in wax-coated chianti bottles, subdued lighting. Specials are on the chalkboard. ♠

Poets have been mysteriously silent on the subject of cheese.

G.K. Chesterton

ENA CHINESE RESTAURANT

432 Ena Road · WAIKIKI
951-0818 · 10am-10pm Daily
VISA, MC · Alcohol Served

Hunan/Szechuan

✧

What is it about tourists that makes them willing to pay good money for lousy food? For reasons unexplained, vacation hot spots like Waikiki (Las Vegas is another dismal example) seem sorrowfully incapable of sustaining decent restaurants—a person can wander for blocks and do no better than an expensive hotel dining room, a Denny's, or some pseudo-ethnic eatery where the food's bland, salty, and overpriced. Blessedly, Ena Restaurant is an unassuming gem of an exception to this rule. Far enough from the main commercial crush of Waikiki to maintain a modicum of integrity, they deign to offer American breakfasts or other similarly depressing inducements.

Eats in the Szechuan and Hunan style reign here, so be ready for a little spice. Like many a Chinese joint, Ena demonstrates the confounding habit of posting hand-written "SPECIAL" signs everywhere; hence, it's often difficult to tell what's what until you realize much of it's simply repetitive. The seafood tends to be superior, and tofu gets pretty fair treatment as well. One particularly cryptic segment of the menu is labeled "Delicate Items," which sounds more like something from a Chinese laundry than a Chinese restaurant. Though sadly devoid of any silken undergarments, it does include dainty offerings like beef with ginger and onion, sweet-and-sour pork, and steak with black pepper sauce.

Noodle dishes here are good and a notch more exciting than those served at most Cantonese places—give the Shanghai chow mein a try. The hot tea is mellow, the service relaxed. The atmosphere is pleasant and comfortable, if a bit unusual. With pink tablecloths, fancy wood paneling, heliotrope walls, and a plenitude

61

of exposed brick, it feels as though it were an upscale pizza parlor in a previous incarnation. Come to think of it, that pretty well describes virtually every restaurant in Waikiki. ♠

Food is heaven to the vulgar masses.
Han Shu, Book of Han

EXPRESSO YOURSELF

900-A Maunakea Street   CHINATOWN
523-5913   9am-3pm Mon-Sat
VISA, MC   No Alcohol

Coffee/Belgian Waffles
✧

Located at the makai end of the Robyn Buntin Galleries (some pretty cool Oriental art, by the by), this place presumably opened as the result of someone deftly deducing that art patrons are not averse to a cappuccino and biscotti now and again.

This lower block of Maunakea is sort of its own little enclave within Chinatown, with several antique shops but nary a restaurant or Asian grocery in evidence. Expresso Yourself is in a handsomely restored building with plenty of brick, wood and glass, and it's the only place in the neighborhood where you can get espresso as such, though you are surrounded by VC (easy there, soldier—that's Vietnamese coffee). The short menu, all of which is available in the small dining area or through the window out front, consists mostly of a few reasonably priced sandwiches and salads ($4-$5) plus java drinks, also fairly priced (a latte runs two bucks, various objets d'art slightly extra). Best bets are the $3.25 Belgian waffle, topped with whipped cream and either bananas, strawberries or pecans, and available anytime, or the scandalously rich espresso shakes. Generally speaking, the coffee is quite good here, though nitpickers be advised that like most everyone else in town they make their lattes too damn foamy. If you can stand the nearly constant drone of traffic from Nimitz Highway, the outdoor patio is a nice place to sip, read, write, draw, chat, relax. ♠

I was determined to know beans.
Henry David Thoreau, Walden

FORT RUGER MARKET

3585 Alohea Avenue   DIAMOND HEAD
737-4531   Plates Served 6:45am-4:30pm Daily
No Plastic   Alcohol for Sale
Hawaiian/Fish Jerky/Poke
✧

    This is among the very best of Oahu's neighborhood markets, and also one of the hardest to find. Located in an otherwise residential neighborhood, Fort Ruger is so low-key that even frequent customers have been known to miss it on the first pass. Do what you have to to find the place, though, as it's well worth the effort.

    Once inside, you'll find they do a lot with a little space. The smell of lau lau is heavy in the air, and shelves are crammed with soap, candy, and sardines; bananas and papayas spill from wooden boxes on the floor. Freshly boiled peanuts are popular with the mostly local clientele, sold in damp paper sacks for about $3 a pound. The line for Hawaiian plates forms to the left as you enter. Various combinations of kalua pig, long rice, poi, lomi salmon and the like go for $4-$6, and they're decent but not remarkable. The real reasons to come here are the poke ($11 per pound)—try the ahi with Maui onion—and the dried and smoked fish jerky. Both the aku and ahi are excellent, but the strips of smoked ono are beyond comparison. Similar in color to dried papaya, these long, leathery strips of fish are rubbed with a bit of salt and cracked pepper; grab a Hawaiian Sun passion fruit nectar from the cooler and you've got an incredible Island snack. Depending on thickness, a six-inch piece of jerky usually costs about $1.50. They also have dried tako (octopus), if you prefer things a little chewier. There's much activity here, what with folks manning the counters and an older gentleman slicing fish behind the counter. A sign above his head reads "Don't complain about the coffee—you might be old and weak yourself someday." ♠

The commoner is satisfied with food and fish.
Hawaiian proverb

FRITZ'S EUROPEAN BAKERY

1336 Dillingham Boulevard
845-0650

KALIHI
7am-6pm Mon-Fri
7am-5pm Sat
"Sundays we rest"

No Plastic

No Alcohol

Bakery
✧

Fritz's is German-owned, and one of the only European-style bakeries in Hawaii. The carpet and chairs are red, and the walls are decorated with pictures of Fritz and his forebears, snappy German sayings, trinkets from the motherland, and several giant lacquered pretzels. Background music is often somber, almost dirge-like. The sandwiches here run around $5; options include Danish ham, turkey breast, Italian salami, Swiss cheese. The best part about them is the bread, made on the premises. Unfortunately, Fritz doesn't offer his most exotic and impressive breads in the sandwich deal. You can only get them by the half or whole loaf ($2.25/$4.50). That may sound a bit steep, but these you've got to see to believe—crusty, cross-hatched beauties like the wheaty westphalia or the dark and delicious bauernbrot. They even have the granddaddy of dense breads, vollkornbrot ($2.90), which weighs about half a pound per slice and is a favorite among Western Europeans for open-faced sandwiches—a little butter, a little cheese, and you're there.

The other baked goods here are of similar quality, always made with butter and fresh cream. The baguette-like rolls are as light as the breads are heavy (a small handwritten sign cryptically declares, "Please do not ask us to butter your rolls—Time is Money") and the various baklavas include chocolate and pecan. There are also delicate cherry tarts with slivered almonds at the edges, chocolate eclairs, apricot turnovers, and Dutch chocolate rum cake. All of these are between 50 cents and $1.50. Meanwhile, out in the parking lot a guy is filling people's propane containers from a huge tank. It's that kind of neighborhood. ♠

He who has butter on his bread should not go into the sun.

Yiddish proverb

64

FU LU SHOU

1451 S. King Street
941-9812
VISA, MC

PAWAA
11am-2pm, 5:30pm-9:30pm Daily
Alcohol Served

Chinese/Indonesian/Thai/Vietnamese

✧

When dining out, a pretty reliable rule of thumb is to be highly suspicious of restaurants offering a variety of cuisines. The jack-of-all-trades, master-of-none routine is considerably more desirable in an apartment building superintendent than it is in a chef. What you want is a specialist. Right?

Well, as it turns out, not always. The folks at Fu Lu Shou attempt to render authentic meals in no less than four genres—Thai, Vietnamese, Indonesian, Chinese—and they achieve a remarkably high rate of success. (Actually, it used to be five, but they dropped the Japanese, and they could probably do the same with the Chinese.) Though the Hinh family is originally from the China side of the Gulf of Tonkin, they lived for years in Vietnam and their food instincts are more Southeast Asian than anything. After successfully launching their multi-cuisine approach to restaurateurship in everybody's favorite test market, Luxembourg, they opened their first Hawaii eatery a few years ago.

Though the interior here is swanky enough to make you wonder, prices are pretty well in line with the competition, if not slightly on the cheap side—$5 for a bowl of pho, with most everything else in the $5-$7 range. Appetizers include one of the best green papaya salads around, slightly sweeter and less garlicky than the norm, with lime, coriander, tomato, red chile and peanuts. Yes, yes, yes. Otherwise, you'll want to check out the sweet sourness of the Indonesian chicken, or the spicy garlic fried fish fillet ($6.25). Vietnamese food fans will be justifiably stoked for the rice paper roll-ups. At $8-$10, these are the priciest item in the house, but outstanding—offerings include grilled beef and shrimp, or chicken brochettes. Service here is excellent, and for dessert there's flan, tapioca, and luscious novelties like fried banana and fried pineapple. ♠

When a man is in great haste he is apt to drink his tea with a fork.

Chinese proverb

GEE...A DELI

418-F Kuulei Road   KAILUA
261-4412
841 Bishop Street   DOWNTOWN
528-3100
10am-7pm Mon-Fri   11am-5pm Sun
10am-6pm Sat   (Downtown hours shorter)
No Plastic   Bring Your Own

Sandwiches
✧

Along with the Hawaiian Cafe, the original Gee...A Deli in Kailua is probably the most difficult-to-find restaurant on the Windward side. Both places haven't exactly benefitted from a recent massive construction project just outside their door. Such is their reputation, though, that business at Gee... continues apace despite the fact that, at first glance, it doesn't appear to be accessible even on foot.

Once on the premises, you'll find a New York-style deli offering a plethora of meats—including four types of salami and four of ham—as well as a dozen or so cheeses. Sandwiches come on either light or dark rye, eight-grain, onion or Kaiser roll. Though you can create your own combo for around $5, most people opt for one of the few dozen colorfully named sandwiches for about the same price. Among the choices are the Evan Aaron Deluxe (patrami, turkey breast, cole slaw, and Russian dressing on an onion roll); the triple-decker club (ham, turkey, bacon, Swiss and cheddar on toasted rye); the wildly popular Sharon's Special (turkey and sweet munchee cheese with lettuce and Russian dressing on an onion roll); and the terrific Gorga Sub (six inches of sturdy, chewy Italian bread layered with hard Italian salami, peppered ham, thin-sliced mozzarella, Italian dressing, and diced pepperoncini). If you like your food to have an especially cryptic moniker, meet the Jack's Texaco Special—roast beef and turkey on an onion roll with a side of slaw.

Though they could stand to be a little larger, the sandwiches here are all very good, and for an extra dollar you can get a side of cole slaw or potato salad. Chips are in the small barrels fronting the counter; in Kailua, there are racks of greeting cards near the door. The TV is always on—usually sports, though their taste is pleasantly eclectic and this is one of the few establishments where you're liable to catch an indoor track meet. Bring your hard hat. ♠

Chew well with your teeth and you'll feel it in your toes.

Meir, Talmud: Sabbath

GOLDEN CROWN CHOP SUEY

46-018 Kam Highway   KANEOHE
235-4505/235-4506   10:30am-9pm Daily
VISA, MC, AMEX   Alcohol Served

Cantonese

Kaneohe isn't generally recognized for its abundance of good eating houses, but it so happens that three of the island's finer chop suey joints are all situated along a two-mile stretch of Kam Highway. Though a cursory glance may suggest that Golden Crown is a clone of its neighbors Kin Wah and Mui Kwai (or vice versa, for the exact genesis of these places is hard to keep track of), they in fact offer the widest variety of the three.

The breadth of the menu is quite impressive, and given the myriad other possibilities chop suey is probably about the last thing you should order. As at Kin Wah, the sizzling platters here are standouts, whether you opt for mixed seafood, chicken or Mongolian beef. They also offer alluring choices like stir-fried scallops and vegetables served in a fried taro nest, a dish that's quite impressive both visually and flavorwise. Taro fans should also give serious thought to Golden Crown's version of taro duck ($6.50).

These folks do up cake noodles in a big way—try the boneless, shoyu-based minute chicken, which along with slender bits of choy sum comes perched atop a platform of noodles for around $6. Also worth serious meditation are the clams in black bean sauce, the stuffed tofu, or the hot pot casseroles (check out the roast duck with lilly flowers and black fungus), as well as virtually any of the daily specials. The majority of these tend to be seafood, usually fish— everything from fried sea bass to salmon in black bean sauce to fresh, chilled New Zealand mullet. Regardless of exoticness, nothing ever exceeds $10, and most of the menu runs in the $5-$7 range. Portions are quite ample. Atmosphere is completely standard for a chop suey house—decrepitude of a pleasant sort, bad lighting, with a few decorations here and there; the main items of interest are the ceiling tiles. These feature a dragon and phoenix, which despite their apparent fierceness actually symbolize good luck. ♠

67

...food is always better eaten in little doleful pinchfuls off the ends of chopsticks, no gobbling, the reason why Darwin's law of survival applies best to China: if you don't know how to handle a chopstick and stick it in that family pot with the best of them, you'll starve.

Jack Kerouac, The Dharma Bums
(1958)

THE GREEK CORNER

1025 University Avenue
942-5503

VISA, MC

MOILIILI
10:30am-10pm Sun-Th
10:30am-11pm Fri-Sat
Alcohol Served

Greek
✧

Though it's not likely to make you think you've died and gone to Athens, this place does serve up some surprisingly decent Greek/Middle Eastern fare. When you're half a planet away from the source in terms of both miles and inclinations, in a town not known for its collective moussaka cravings, you've got to take it where you find it. And this is one of the only sources around, just down the street from UH between a sushi shop and a plate lunch joint.

Though they have indoor tables covered with green- and white-striped tablecloths, The Greek Corner is primarily a takeout spot. The owners prefer to stick to the mother tongue as much as possible and the kitchen where they whip up gyros, souvlaki, and baba ghanouj is, dimensionally speaking, something you might find in a Waikiki studio, with the notable ad- dition of a grill, an extra refrigerator, and cigarettes intended for resale. There's little else to say on the at-mosphere count, other than one gets the vague notion that revolutions are hatched in places like this.

The menu reads thisaway: gyros run about $4.50 and are made with either a beef and lamb mixture or chicken, both of which are great. For the same money you can get pita pockets filled with stiff, paprika-dusted hummus, smooth baba ghanouj (a specialty), or felafel, which is made with both chick peas and fava beans, and laced with cumin. It's not too dry, very nice. Full plates include souvlaki and dolmades (stuffed grape leaves), as well as the afore-mentioned items, but they are a bit steep given the modest portions. These folks also pride themselves on their spanakopita, and for dessert there's (surprise!) baklava. ♠

There's something I've noticed about food: whenever there's a crisis if you can get people to eating normally things get better.

Madeleine L'Engle, The Moon by Night

HA BIEN

198 N. King Street   CHINATOWN
531-1185/524-5991   8am-4pm Daily
VISA, MC   Bring Your Own

Vietnamese

✧

The 15 or so tables at Ha Bien are packed snugly, and the air conditioning is usually cranked. Otherwise, things are just as most American diners would like: clean, bright, safe, and alas, rather uninteresting. As for the food, it's not only consistently fresh and damn delicious, but there's also plenty of it. Appetizers are compe-tent interpretations of standards like green papaya salad, spring rolls, and minty, resilient rice paper rolls ($2.50).

Here, as with most Vietnamese places, the choicest items come in a bowl. Predictably, pho is a main attraction, but it's hardly the lone option of interest—besides, To Chau next door serves the de-finitive rendition. Ha Bien shows particular acumen with soups not always seen in Vietnamese eateries—witness the dashingly hand-some look fun with seafood, a veritable stocked pond of shrimp, squid, and fishball; the noodles with steamed duck; and the long rice with crabmeat and shrimp. Dry noodle dishes (bun) are also sensational, particularly the spring roll and grilled pork version. Here we find our heroes shamelessly sprawled on a bed of slender rice noodles, begging to be doused with sweet sauce. Also superb for the non-soup-eater are the crispy-fried noodles topped with a zingy melange of beef, shrimp, and vegetables (at around $6, one of the priciest dishes they serve). The rice plates are something of an Achilles heel and probably best avoided.

69

Also worthy of mention are the beverages, which include Mix Drink (described as "translucent seaweed with pomegranate and bean and coconut milk") and fresh lemonade. The Vietnamese iced coffee is particularly comely. You mix it yourself, and though it pours like another Elly May Clampett breakfast endeavor gone horribly awry, it is, in fact, exquisite, and sufficiently packed with caffeine as to allow you to hear yourself blinking for the next 12 hours or so. ♠

The green limes that I gathered were not only pleasant to eat but very wholesome; and I mixed their juice afterwards with water, which made it very wholesome and very cool and refreshing.

Daniel Defoe, Robinson Crusoe

HAJJIBABA'S

4614 Kilauea Avenue   KAHALA
735-5522   6pm-10pm Daily
VISA, MC, AMEX   Alcohol Served

Moroccan

✧

Strictly speaking, bargain eateries aren't always defined by cost alone. And though Hajjibaba's prices blatantly exceed cheap eating parameters, it nonetheless deserves mention as both an exceptional deal for the money and a singular dining experience, atmospherically and gastronomically, for which no other Island restaurant can prepare you. Hard by Kahala Mall, the ambience is as seductively Arabian as one can expect from a place that shares parking with a Subway: stacked ottomans, Persian rugs and perimeter couches. Cushions abound should you prefer lounging on the floor. Even the lighting bespeaks romance, and there's usually a belly dancer on duty. The waiters provide excellent service, attentive but by no means intrusive. These fellows are pros, with an interesting, knowing air, more like accomplices than servers. Their stylish manner is further augmented by raiments downright dashing—white, collarless jackets and matching pants with a voluminous, knee-reaching crotch that may help you envision just how someone goes about shoplifting a microwave. Red skullcaps complete the ensemble.

Though items are available a la carte, most diners opt for one of five feasts ranging in price from $18 to $35 a person. Meals commence with a brief hand-washing ceremony, followed promptly by harira soup—a smooth, tomato-lentil combo. Then come the salads, either Moroccan (marinated carrots, eggplant, tomatoes and peppers) or Tangier (hummus, tabouli, baba ghanouj). These are absolutely gorgeous and beyond reproach in terms of quality. The vegetarian feast comes with all of these, radiating outward from a nucleus of basil leaves and ripe olives. Sans utensils, you'll be freehanding it with the aid of fine, sturdy bread. Next item is the flaky pastilla, phyllo pastry stuffed with saffron chicken and almonds, dusted with cinnamon and powdered sugar. Luscious to be sure, but also exceedingly rich, so tread lightly. Meat options include chicken and plenty of lamb, and the tagine of fish (swordfish baked with tomatoes, peppers, lemon, and olives) is indicative of a nice touch with seafood. Skewered lamb brochettes are also prime, very minty and slyly hot. Couscous, a Moroccan staple, accompanies every feast; though attractive, it's less interesting than the other dishes. Things wind down with hot mint tea, sweet and refreshing. It's pouring, like everything else here, is done with a flourish. Lastly comes a ceremonial sprinkling of orange blossom water. Meals are extended and luxuriant, best experienced when you have no timetable for the evening. Frankincense and myrrh accepted as payment. ♠

To be without a sense of taste is to be deficient in an exquisite faculty, that of appreciating the qualities of food, just as a person may lack the faculty of appreciating the quality of a book or a work of art. It is to want a vital sense, one of the elements of human superiority.

Guy de Maupassant

HALE VIETNAM

1140 12th Avenue   KAIMUKI

735-7581   10am-10pm Mon-Sat

                                                10am-9pm Sun

VISA, MC   Alcohol Served

Vietnamese

✧

The results of a 1992 facelift are clearly in evidence: expanded seating, muted interior tones of charcoal and light gray, abundant foliage, and some fairly terrific watercolor murals. Though larger than most Vietnamese eateries, Hale Vietnam feels more intimate. With the exception of the very fine pho (offered in no less than 17 formats and priced at the universal ceiling of $5), expect to pay a couple bucks more per item here than in Chinatown. Virtually across the board, quality is exemplary and portions are often huge.

Outstanding appetizers include summer rolls (shrimp, pork, herbs and lettuce in rice paper) and the vegetarian temple rolls (yam, potato, and tofu taking the place of meat)—both served with titillatingly complex dipping sauces—as well as the deep-fried imperial rolls, meant to be wrapped in a fresh lettuce leaf with noodles and herbs. Salads are a tad spendy ($7.25) but definitely impressive—try the lemon-beef made with charbroiled slices of steak, or the green papaya salad with shrimp. Curries are another strong area, available with beef, chicken, seafood, or no meat at all. The yellow has the more pronounced coconut flavor, while the green is redolent of green chiles and aromatic herbs. Bun (thin rice noodles) are also top-notch and available with a choice of meats, beautifully garnished with toasted peanuts, onion flakes, coriander and mint (around $6.50). ♠

Wine and meat attract many friends.
Chinese proverb

HAMBURGER MARY'S ORGANIC GRILL
2109 Kuhio Avenue   WAIKIKI
922-6722   7am-12am Daily (bar open until 2am)
VISA, MC, AMEX   Alcohol Served

Burgers

✧

In a sea of neon, asphalt, and slick self-promotion, Hamburger Mary's is a very inviting place. It has the comfortable, relaxed look one rarely sees in Waikiki, except in caricatured form. Somehow, Mary's manages to pull off the grass shack theme with unusual aplomb. There's plenty of wood and bamboo and the interior's festooned with gewgaws of every dimension, everything from a child's bicycle to a souvenir plate from Bemidji, Minnesota. The outdoor dining area is cordoned from the sidewalk by tropical plants and a massive shade tree. Though some tourists remain oblivious to the preponderance of nattily attired men dining in pairs here, Mary's is locally regarded as the finest gay bar on the island—ditto on Maui, where there's a Mary's in downtown Wailuku—as well as home to some pretty fair eats.

The menu is neither large nor terribly inexpensive (remember where you are, after all), but the food is promising and the service good. It also has the added appeal of being an excellent place to kick back and chat on a sunny afternoon. As you might expect, burgers get star billing here, and they're served on buns, multi-grain bread or sweet bread; the last of these you'll want to skip as it's completely ill-suited to sandwich applications. Burgers start at $4.25 and run to $7.50 for the double patty Diamond Head Burger, which includes veggies and a major slab of cream cheese, all piled into a 6-inch stack. The $2 home fries are good, as is the iced tea, often botched in these parts. Meatless options include garden burgers and things like Vegetarian Benedict; other sandwiches of note are turkey and the mahi with mustard dressing, though you'll need to watch for bones. One of the most popular items is called Our Famous Chili Size—a burger topped with heavy-duty chili, onions, and cheese. $6.50 buys what's called the light load, with the full load running a buck more. ♠

Nothing ever tasted any better than a cold beer on a beautiful afternoon with nothing to look forward to but more of the same.
Hugh Hood

73

HAN YANG

1311 N. King Street   KALIHI
845-3513   9am-10pm Daily
VISA, MC   Alcohol Served

Korean

✧

    Korean food has a certain omnipresence in Honolulu, and folks in the working-class environs of Kalihi do the kim chee thang at Han Yang, in business for the last decade. Tucked in a ragtag shopping center just across from Helena's Hawaiian Food, this place looks perpetually closed, what with the blinds drawn and all. Once inside, one discovers a spacious place, replete with mirrors, hand-lettered signs, and the sort of red leatherette booths found at Italian restaurant foreclosure sales. The menu is fairly sizable and a bit confusing to the uninitiated so it'll behoove you to ask for guidance from the cheerful staff, most of whom do a nice job of explaining things provided of course you speak Korean. Otherwise, plan on doing a lot of pointing, gesturing and nodding.

    Korean chow is quite distinctive and certainly not for the faint-of-palate, but most of the offerings here are quite exemplary. Bi bim bap, a traditional fave, is ample and quite mouth-watering. Rice is served on the side with most entrees, and meant to be combined with the various condiments and kim chees that make Korean dining such a blast. Pickled cucumber and daikon frequently appear, as do spicy fried tofu, seaweed, sesame-inflected soy sprouts, and so on—some tame, some fiery, all tasty. Should you be considering soups, be advised that the fish soups are very fishy, and all things brothy are served just this side of the boiling point. ♠

Soup and fish explain half of the emotions of life.
Sydney Smith

HATA

1742 S. King Street   PAWAA
941-2686   10:30am-2pm, 5pm-9pm Mon-Sat
No Plastic   Bring Your Own

Japanese

✧

Part of what makes Hata initially interesting is the way it seemingly tries its dead-level best to remain unnoticed. Their sign is dinky, their windows covered; the lone attempt at advertising consists of photos depicting various meals, but unfortunately time and the tropical sun have bleached these to a sickly gold and you can't discern much beyond the vague image of a bowl. The inside is a bit more engaging, with chilly A/C, perhaps a dozen small tables, and at least five calendars in evidence (including one saluting sumo stars, big-boned local boys among them). As always, ignore the American side of the menu and instead devote your full attention to Japanese standouts like tonkatsu, udon, chicken cutlet, or the good-to-go mixed tempura, featuring ahi and vegetables for an al- together reason-able $5.75. They also serve ozoni, the mochi soup tradi- tionally eaten at New Year's. It's packed with vegetables and a lightly cooked egg, brought to your table in a steaming black cauldron that might well recall the opening credits of *Kung Fu*.

Otherwise, keep a close eye on the hand-written daily specials, most of which are seafood: salmon teriyaki, ahi belly (that's prime cut), fried opakapaka, oysters. These are usually very fine and run in the $7-$8 range. For noodle freaks, there's saimin and rahmen. Everything is served with lotiony-tasting tsukemono on the side. ♠

There is one almost infallible way to find honest food at just prices in blue-highway America: count the wall calendars in a cafe.

> *No calendar: Same as interstate pit stop.*
> *One calendar: Preprocessed food assembled in New Jersey.*
> *Two calendar: Only if fish trophies present.*
> *Three calendar: Can't miss on the farm-boy breakfasts.*
> *Four calendar: Try the ho-made pies too.*
> *Five calendar: Keep it under your hat, or they'll franchise.*

William Least Heat Moon, Blue Highways (1982)

HAWAIIAN BAGEL

753-B Halekauwila Street   KAKAAKO
523-8638   6am-3:30pm Mon-Th
                                                      6am-5:30pm Fri
                                                       6am-3pm Sat
No Plastic   No Alcohol

Bagels
✧

Here's proof positive that Honolulu has to rank with the top American cities in terms of being able to sustain an amazing number of gastronomically diverse establishments. Where else on the planet, after all, can you find poi, chitlins, pad thai, *and* a decent pumpernickel bagel, all within a few miles of each other?

Hawaiian Bagel is actually close to Ala Moana Center and Waikiki, but you wouldn't know it by the neighborhood. Located on a dusty street in the warehouse-industrial district of Kakaako, it's surrounded by enterprises which rely heavily on the use of loud power tools. Since 1980 it has been Honolulu's lone source of quality bagels, courtesy of New York transplants the Gelsons.

The bagels here are very good: sturdy, resilient, not at all bready, with a slightly crunchy exterior distinct from the softer interior. They come 12 ways—blueberry, cinnamon-raisin, Hawaiian salt, even oat bran—and cost 45 cents apiece ($5 and change for a dozen). Prices drop by more than half for day-old goods, frequently available in the mornings. Most of the bagels in area restaurants and coffeehouses come from here, but nobody serves them fresher or cheaper. Bagels with spreads run about $1.25 to $2; whether it's cream cheese and lox, raisin-walnut, or peanut butter and honey, they load it on. They also bake muffins, croissants, and loaves of New York rye and the traditional Jewish egg bread known as challah that are to die for.

Also a deli, they offer sandwiches—chopped liver, smoked turkey, kosher salami, pastrami, corned beef, this type of thing—for under $5. Other Jewish staples include potato knishes, pickled herring, and Dr. Brown's Cream Soda. The setting is unremarkable but spacious, with plenty of room to lounge around and read the paper or scan the latest issue of *Hawaii Jewish News*. Or grab it to go and head around the corner to the neighborhood's other hidden gem, Lion Coffee. ♠

I eat out maybe 360 days a year. It's just something I enjoy doing.

Woody Allen

HAWAIIAN CAFE

417 Uluniu Street   KAILUA
263-4852   11am-3pm Mon-Fri (closed holidays)
VISA, MC   No Alcohol

Hawaiian

Generally speaking, authentic Hawaiian food is served in buildings seemingly bound for a date with the wrecking ball. Though they definitely serve the genuine article, newcomer Hawaiian Cafe is housed in a decidedly atypical setting. Finding them can be a chore, and you're history without the address—it's in the rear of a small professional building (this is essentially a dentist's office with a stove) and there's no sign. The nearest neighbor is a gastroenterologist—sheer coincidence, rest assured. The food's terrific. Really.

Walls are beige grasscloth, with a few paintings of the pali and the Mokes, plus a couple of Gauguin prints from his days spent laying among the Polynesian ladies. Meals are about $6, and offer a bit of variation on the standard Hawaiian themes. Notable deviations include the ahi poke and the chicken lau lau, made with moist white meat. The pipikaula is especially appetizing—it's fried like bacon and served hot, crispy at the edges. A large side order is $2. The haupia here is creamier and better than most. By the way, that bottle of Molokai Hot Sauce you see is quite lethal, not to be confused with the usual chile water. ♠

I think there must be as much of a knack in handling poi as there is in eating with chopsticks. The forefinger is thrust into the mess and stirred quickly round several times and drawn as quickly out, just as if it were poulticed; the head is thrown back, the finger inserted in the mouth, and the delicacy stripped off and swallowed—the eye closing gently, meanwhile, in a languid sort of ecstasy.

Mark Twain, Mark Twain in Hawaii
(1866)

HELENA'S HAWAIIAN FOOD

1364 N. King Street   KALIHI
845-8044   11am-7:30pm Tue-Fri
No Plastic   No Alcohol

Hawaiian

✧

In business since 1946, Helena's is a local institution with a much-deserved reputation for the best Hawaiian food on the island. Helena and her cohorts, many of them kindly women on the north side of 60, run a tight ship, and quality is a given here. Like many a fine cheap restaurant, Helena's is the height of unpretentiousness: a ramshackle building, simple wooden booths, thick plastic dishes identical to those used in elementary schools. Add in several fine works by renowned local artist Jean Charlot, and you have the sort of authentic air that other places spend tens of thousands of dollars trying futilely to manufacture.

Helena's serves landmark versions of favorites like lau lau, kalua pig, chicken long rice, squid luau, poke (with opihi, even) and fried ahi that's a must. Though complete plates including poi and homemade haupia sell for $5-$6, the a la carte menu is alarmingly inexpensive; if you're the adventurous sort, it's best to simply order whatever strikes your fancy. The day-old poi is nice and tangy, and they also offer a couple of rarely-seen local delicacies, naaupua (large intestine) and ake (raw liver), both something of a dubious bargain at around $1.75. ♠

Native Hawaiian cooking has tended to become lost in the influx of foreign foods, except as a folklore spectacle staged for tourists, a development which, in most of the countries where it has occurred, has resulted in adulteration of the individuality of characteristic local cuisines, since their most salient features are almost automatically the least acceptable to visitors from other cultures, and accordingly are watered down to appeal to outsiders.

Waverley Root and **Richard de Rochemont**, Eating in America (1976)

HIGHWAY INN

94-226 Leoku Street   WAIPAHU
677-4345   7am-2:30pm Mon-Sat
                        5pm-8pm Wed-Fri
No Plastic   No Alcohol

Hawaiian

✧

The back of their takeout menu bears the phone number for an enterprise called Makahari Hawaii Dojo. Also included is a cryptic explanation of how makahari (Japanese for *divine light*) acts as a purgative of sorts, gathering toxins accumulated from the environment so they can be "eliminated from the body in a natural way." While you may question the wisdom of placing such an ad on a menu jammed with meat—or any menu for that matter—you'll be far less likely to doubt the quality of the Hawaiian grinds here.

The bill of fare is divided into American and Hawaiian sections. While the former is nothing you haven't seen a hundred times before, the Hawaiian food is better and more eclectic. Besides one of the meatiest, tastiest lau lau around, they offer wet and dry pipikaula (wet's like stew meat, dry's like very cooked tenderloin), butterfish in stew gravy, and huakai egg soup. Besides Helena's, Highway Inn is one of the few places around offering naaupua, made with intestines and taro and not likely to hold much appeal for the non-kamaaina. Considerably more likely to transcend culturally conditioned preferences is the lomi aku, made fresh and served with a few ice cubes to keep it cold. You'll have to show up early, as it disappears in a hurry.

Highway Inn is a bit tricky, pricewise. Most places offer Hawaiian plates in the $5-$8 range, but here everything is a la carte. Though portions are decent, it's not all that hard to run up a bill of over $10, as most everything other than rice and poi costs $3-$4. What with all the car dealerships and discount stores, Waipahu isn't much acclaimed for its atmosphere. The Highway Inn is at one end of a dismal little shopping complex; its interior is small and pretty nondescript, characterized primarily by the strains of AM 1420, the best station on Oahu for traditional Hawaiian music. ♠

Eat standing, eat walking.
Hawaiian proverb

HONG LINH ORIENTAL SEED CENTER

1041 Kekaulike Street   CHINATOWN
531-7782   8am-5pm Mon-Sat
                                  8am-2pm Sun
No Plastic   No Alcohol

Crack Seed
✧

Located just behind the main bus stop on Hotel Street (across from the Maunakea Marketplace), this inconspicuous establishment is made all the more so thanks to a sign that's been partially smashed. Facing from Hotel Street it's on your left, and worth investigating, as they sell some of the best and least expensive crack seed on the island.

Like any crack seed joint worth its salt, Hong Linh displays its products in glass jars huge enough to put your head in—though I certainly don't condone that sort of thing. They also sell sodas, cigarettes, and fresh fruit, but crack seed's why you come here, and they have it in spades. A multi-tiered island of jars dominates the center of the store, with more lining the walls. The most common item is li hing mui, a preserved plum that's usually both salty and sweet. It's offered in dizzying variety—red, brown, dry, wet (unlike most places, they don't use saccharine for this one)—you name it. They also have sweet and sour apricots and peaches, red papaya, dried mango with licorice, several types of lemon peel, mochi crunch, apple seed, cuttlefish, dried abalone. You begin to get the idea.

First-timers may find themselves a bit intimidated by the selection, and the owners aren't usually much help beyond a yes or no. Take your time, check it out, and take solace in the fact that it's all quality stuff. Most items run around $2.50 the quarter pound, which is as small as they'll go. Experiment. ♠

The mouth should always consult with the stomach.
Chinese proverb

HOUSE OF PARK'S CAFE

2671-D S. King Street   MOILIILI
949-2679   11am-8:30pm Mon-Sat
VISA, MC   Bring Your Own

Korean

✧

House of Park's isn't particularly roomy, though the seating arrangements are—expansive, comfy booths, the tabletops inlaid with mother-of-pearl moons and swooping cranes. The one bad seat in the house is beneath the air conditioner; at best you'll wind up with damp hair, while more paranoid diners will feel certain the annoying droplets could only be the work of those gutless bastards at the next table. The decor is best described as mixed-media: linoleum, painted-over windows, pressed-wood paneling, those mirrored tiles with the gold marbling.

The menu consists primarily of soups and barbecue plates. The kim chee is homemade, and everything pickled cabbage should be—not too salty, slightly crunchy but by no means raw, hot but not paralyzingly so. Best of the hot soups is the man doo, a stuffed dumpling that's a kissing cousin to the Chinese won ton; they're served in a virtual vat of chicken broth, bobbing to the surface like hungry carp. Also interesting are the less common chilled soups. The cold kuk soo is certainly worth investigating, though probably not for everyone. Served in a large steel bowl, it features rice noodles swimming in clear daikon broth, topped with barbecue beef, shredded carrot, cucumber, and green onion, plus a few ice cubes. Minus the beef it makes a nice option for vegetarians—something of a rara avis in a Korean restaurant.

Beef, kal bi (short ribs), and chicken are the main non-soup attractions, offered solo and in various combinations, with prices topping out at about $6. Plates come with rice, kim chee and other vegetables. Though all the meats are reputable at minimum, the spicy chicken approaches genius quality. Boneless, skinless bird is grilled with care, but only after some hard minutes in a fiendishly hot red bean sauce that's without peer in this town. Despite the caliber of the eats, crowds are rarely a problem. Parking, however, is a different story, especially during weekdays. Service is generally very attentive except on Sundays, when they're closed. ♠

The red pepper, though small, is hot.
Korean proverb

HUEVOS

Off Kam Highway (look for the purple sign) KAHUKU
No Phone 7am-12pm Th-Mon
No Plastic No Alcohol

Breakfast
✧

There's something about finding greatness where you least expect it that kindles the appetite. This is especially true, of course, with regard to restaurants; for the adventurous eater, there's no rush quite like stumbling upon a jewel in the wilderness. And Huevos is definitely such a place, hidden down a dirt lane just past the old sugar mill as you head toward Laie. Save for a small sign out by the road, you'd have no reason to suspect there's a restaurant nestled in what looks like, and is, a sleepy cluster of residences.

Huevos is in a wonderful old building that was once a Japanese bathhouse. At various other times it served as a store and a private residence before being converted to a restaurant nearly a decade ago. Since then, it has garnered an underground reputation for cheap, hearty breakfasts that are the rival of any on the island. The menu is handwritten in the Moosewood style, and it's fairly simple: basically eggs (with choice of meats), omelettes, or a nice veggie stir-fry for ovo-lacto abstainers. These all run in the $5-$7.50 range and are quite substantial, served with rice or potatoes (a heap of seasoned home fries) and toast or pancakes (definitely the pancakes). They also have sweet bread French toast for under $4, and fresh fruit.

Eating here is always a treat, sort of like going to a friends house to grind. The interior is actually two good-sized rooms, the decor a mellow blend of antiqueish Island charm and gentle hippie purpleness, punctuated by the sound of vegetables being chopped and the easy lilt of Hawaiian tunes, mostly traditional stuff. ♠

All happiness depends on a leisurely breakfast.
John Gunther (1958)

HUONG LAN

100 N. Beretania Street   CHINATOWN
538-6707   8am-5pm Daily
VISA, MC   Bring Your Own

Vietnamese

✧

This is the mauka edge of Chinatown, where the run-down, two-story buildings give way to high-rise apartment buildings shining like stalagmites in the sun. There's a different feel out here on the perimeter, and Huong Lan is surrounded by small shops primarily of interest only if you're a fan of Vietnamese pop music or a misguided tourist seeking personalized jade elephants in a variety of sizes. Though they offer other things, this is essentially a pho shop, as evidenced by the fact that everyone here is Vietnamese, and that's what they're all having. There's a time to be a maverick, and a time to follow the herd—pho it is.

Huong Lan's broth is nigh on boiling, which works well if you opt for the delicacy of choice, rare steak on the side. Though the pho isn't unimpeachable, it's awfully good, and both the appearance and portions of their steak puts them in a league with Honolulu's soup elite. To be truly Vietnamese about it, one carefully swabs the meat with hoisin and sriracha, adding perhaps a dash of white pepper and a splash of fish sauce. Then into the broth they go, along with herbs, sprouts, chiles and a healthy squirt of lemon. This, my friends, is good living.

The decor is inoffensive but not particularly thrilling. Besides the obligatory Vietnam-shaped clock, there are green booths, ceiling fans, and music that sounds oddly reminiscent of early-70's James Bond themes thumping in from the shop next door. Service is indifferent but adequate. Bowls are around $5, and recommended beverages include iced coffee with condensed milk (a bargain at $1.50) and the fresh-squeezed OJ ($2.50, blended with a fresh egg for 45 cents more). ♠

Happiness is for me largely a matter of digestion.
Lin Yutang

83

I LOVE COUNTRY CAFE

451 Piikoi Street   ALA MOANA
526-3927   10:30am-9pm Mon-Fri
                                                   10:30am-8pm Sat
                                                    11am-5pm Sun
No Plastic   No Alcohol

Sandwiches/Salads/Stir-Frys
✧

Here we have an excellent example of the sort of mixed-metaphor eatery common to Hawaii, a natural outgrowth of the Islands' diverse cultural make-up. Though it bears precious little resemblance—atmospherically or foodwise—to a country cafe of the traditional, checked tablecloth ilk, they do a nice job of delivering wholesome, tasty food inspired by disparate influences.

Themes here include vegetarian, local plate lunch, Chinese, down-home, and fern bar (things like fried cheese, which you can easily skip). Salads are fresh and in the $4 range; sandwiches are substantial—meatloaf, roast turkey straight from the bird—and run upwards of $5. The Philadelphia cheese steaks are made to order and quite respectable. Specials include a nice stir-fry and turkey and dressing. They get pretty jammed at lunch, what with the folks from nearby offices and shoppers from Ala Moana Center; despite the crush, the stoic cook stands at the grill, never harried, rarely speaking, scarcely glancing at the throng that surrounds him. There are only five small tables inside—better to sit outside or get it to go. Most everything is in the $4-$6 range, and service is cheerful and amazingly quick. The setting is hardly what can be described as the boondocks: a pretty forgettable strip mall that's also home to a Blockbuster video store and an I Can't Believe It's Yogurt. Yikes. ♠

Kissing don't last; cookery do.
George Meredith

IMPERIAL SEAFOOD PALACE

1010 University Avenue   MOILIILI
944-8838   10:30am-2am Daily
VISA, MC   Alcohol Served

Cantonese

Tucked rather inconspicuously behind Rainbow Books, Imperial is unusually open and bright for a Chinese restaurant, with plenty in the way of obligatory dragons and red tablecloths. A sizable portion of the back wall is tanks of lobsters and crabs, tangled and groping like a scene from the glory days at Hef's mansion. And notice please the background music: traditional Chinese tunes intermingled with Muzaked Stevie Wonder and the *Star Trek* theme. After you, Mr. Sulu.

Appetizers run the range, from the omnipresent egg rolls and fried gau gee to a shrimp and fruit salad, marinated cold jellyfish, and the excellent deep-fried stuffed tofu—crispy outside, silky inside. Most dishes here are Cantonese; freshness is never a concern, but spiciness, or rather the lack thereof, can be. If you like things with some zip, stick to the starred items. This is where Imperial shines, and it's also an effective way of whittling the lengthy menu to more manageable dimensions.

The hot and sour soup is a blast—tangy, complex, and well-stocked. If someone else is paying, splurge on lobster or Dungeness crab; for something more affordable (the vast majority of dishes are under $7), try the calamari with curry sauce or the barely sweet Scallop Honey Walnut. Eggplant with garlic sauce is probably the best dish in the house, made with bamboo shoots, shredded pork and black mushrooms. Red chile and ginger add a touch of heat and the right amount of pucker. Non-meat-eaters should try the cold tofu with a dark and zingy sesame sauce. Be advised that the term *vegetarian* is used here in the loosest of senses, with some dishes so labeled containing dried fish and oyster sauce; make sure you ask. Noodles are disappointing, and Imperial also serves jook, the traditional rice gruel. It's the Cantonese equivalent of poi or grits, which is to say appealing mainly to those who grew up on the stuff. After 9 p.m., they offer a nice and inexpensive shabu shabu. Meat, seafood, and noodles are poached fondue-style in boiling chicken broth; key to the operation is the dipping sauce, a subtle yet delicious fusion of peanut oil, shredded ginger, scallion, soy, sesame and vinegar. ♠

Out in the garden in the moonlight, our servant is scraping a golden carp with so much vigor that the scales fly in every direction—perhaps they go as high as heaven. Those beautiful stars up there might be the scales of our fish.

Author unknown (Chinese), Before the Repast

INDIA BAZAAR MADRAS CAFE

2320 S. King Street   MOILIILI
949-4840   11am-9pm Mon-Sat
No Plastic   Bring Your Own

Indian

Stashed away in a small shopping center near UH, India Bazaar's high-ceilinged interior is a relaxed combination of lovely print table-cloths, travel posters of the motherland, and artworks heavy on both elephants and sitars. One wall is devoted to grocery items—spices, biryani sauce, mango chutney, chile pickle—and the odor is quite invigorating.

The menu here's small and for the most part straightforward, and meals are served in large stainless steel pans that look like something out of *Cool Hand Luke*. Pakoras (the Indian equivalent to tempura) and samosas (stuffed turnovers) both run less than $1, and you'll find a choice of six entrees, all served with a memorable spiced Indian rice that's loaded with roasted mustard seed and other tiny crunchies. The vegetable thali is a selection of three curries, and all the meat offerings are high-grade, with the mahi masala and the succulent, coriander-laced chicken tikka particularly noteworthy. Curry selections vary somewhat, but it's hard to go awry. The coconut cauliflower korma is creamy and mild, the chole (curried chick peas) spicier but not overwhelming, and the coconut curry vegetables are fantastic. Dals are also tasty and generally on the mild side, though they sometimes use whole dried chiles that can have caustic repercussions should you inadvertently bite down on one. Chapatis (crisp Indian flat bread), yogurt raitas, and lassi, an excellent yogurt beverage, are also available. Entrees run in the vicinity of $6, and portions are substantial, slightly less so if you go the takeout route. ♠

If you ask the hungry man how much is two and two, he replies four loaves.
Hindu proverb

IRIFUNE

563 Kapahulu Avenue   KAPAHULU
737-1141   11:30am-1:30pm, 5pm-9:30pm Tue-Fri
                                          5pm-9:30pm Sat-Sun
VISA, MC   Bring Your Own

Japanese
✧

Though less than a mile from Waikiki, Irifune stands light years distant from most of that district's Japanese restaurants in terms of both value and authenticity. The place is hardly pretentious: on the walls are Japanese masks, calendars, plaudits from both English and Japanese publications, paper fans, fish charts and artist's renderings of Mount Fuji. There is no plastic food in sight. The wooden tables are small and simple, the chairs of the fold-up variety.

The owners are brothers Hitoshi and Mitsuo Ishizawa, a pair of headband-sporting cooks with garlic on their minds. They offer udon and curries, as well as some pretty fair tempura. Other specialties include barbecue chicken and teriyaki beef, a wonderful ahi spinach salad, and some fine sashimi. Fans of the clove are hereby steered in the direction of the garlic ahi, crab, or shrimp. Meals are served according to the Japanese culinary paradigm, which deems American-sized portions nothing short of vulgar. Instead, there are many little things—outstanding miso soup, mild pickled daikon, rice, and assorted condiments, everything in its own little dish. With few exceptions, prices are in the $7-$8 range. Lunch is never crowded, but weekend evenings can be a different story—no problem, for they have a comfortable waiting area replete with old magazines, odd recliners, even a rattan daybed should you feel the need to get horizontal. ♠

Who could ever weary of moonlit nights and well-cooked rice?
Japanese proverb

87

ISLAND MANAPUA FACTORY

Manoa Marketplace   MANOA
988-5441
Inside Shirokiya   ALA MOANA CENTER
973-9238
811 Gulick Avenue (factory)   KALIHI
847-2677
8:30am-8pm Mon-Sat   8:30am-5pm Sun (hours vary)
No Plastic   No Alcohol

Cantonese/Manapua

Despite their sizable wholesale business, Island Manapua is essentially a Chinese takeout joint like most any other, at least in terms of appearance and atmosphere. And though Hawaii suffers no dearth of this type of establishment, Island Manapua ranks as one of the best in town in terms of both quality and value.

Though the Manoa enterprise is rather miniscule, able to seat maybe ten people—the Shirokiya outlet has no seating at all—the menu is surprisingly diverse. Large soups (most around $4) include pork with mustard cabbage and seaweed versions; main dishes range from spicy pork tofu to chicken with eggplant (both under $5) to perhaps the cheapest Peking duck around ($5.50). If you're into it, the chicken with bitter melon is a particularly credible version. Should you wish to go the combination route, you can get any three entrees plus a heap of fried rice or noodles (get the chow fun) for less than $4. A hellacious deal, really.

Island Manapua also offers manapua, of course, as well as numerous other articles of dim summery. The stuffed buns rate with Honolulu's heavyweights, and for about 75 cents a pop they can be had steamed or baked. Of the fillings, char siu and the chicken (with curry or oyster sauce) are the ones to nab. The pork hash dumplings and the half moons also have their followings. A number of the sweets are worthwhile, particularly the jin dui (poofy, chewy balls filled with sticky rice and coconut). ♠

The flavors are only five in number but their blends are so various that one cannot taste them all.
Sun-Tzu, The Art of War (@ 350 B.C.)

JA JA

1210 Dillingham Boulevard   KALIHI
842-5695   10:30am-2:30pm, 5pm-10pm Wed-Mon
VISA, MC   Bring Your Own

Northern Chinese

✧

Welcome to the Kapalama Shopping Center, a cluster of businesses far more interesting than it looks. It's actually a pretty fair example of complex Island gastronomy in microcosm, with a Zippy's, a great Korean supermarket, a local plate lunch joint, and Ja Ja, a Taiwanese-owned eatery specializing in Northern Chinese cuisine.

Despite it's lack of exterior promise, the interior at Ja Ja is pleasant and comfortable, the food of consistent merit and priced

right. Most any of the
trusted, and the dry-
spicy, and downright
ball soup, made with
choice for diners look-
rizons a bit; Lovers of
while, should find hap-
antly gooey Shanghai
mented by assorted veg-
dards go, the kung pao
this oft-bungled dish
dark red chiles, crisp
pepper, peanuts, and
and succulent. The
etables is tasty, awash
sauce. Ja Ja is an espe-
vegetarians, in fact, as
tensive list of dishes
meat, i.e., wheat gluten
in place of animal
vised by Buddhist
thing runs in the $5-$7
table exception being
served in a sealed

noodle dishes can be
fried chicken is sticky,
excellent. Dry squid
fresh fish cake, is a nice
ing to expand their ho-
glutinous rice, mean-
piness with the pleas-
mochi cake, aug-
etables. As far as stan-
chicken is everything
should be: plenty of
water chestnuts, bell
chicken that's tender
Hunan tofu with veg-
in a spicy black bean
cially safe haven for
they offer a fairly ex-
made with meatless
and soybean skins used
flesh—an idea first de-
monks. Most every-
range, with the one no-
Beggar's Chicken,
earthen crock. It's so

named because in centuries past, impoverished chefs who lacked a proper cooking vessel would simply wrap the bird in mud and set it in an open blaze. It costs $22 and requires one day's advance notice, but it's an experience worth the hassle and expense. ♠

89

My new province is a land of bamboo groves:
Their shoots in spring fill the valleys and hills...
I put the shoots in a great earthen pot
And heat them up along with boiling rice.
The purple nodules broken—like an old brocade;
The white skin opened—like new pearls.
Now every day I eat them recklessly...

Po Chu-I (772-846 A.D.), "Eating Bamboo Shoots"

JANE'S FOUNTAIN

1719 Liliha Street   LILIHA
533-1238   6am-10pm Mon-Fri
                                                       7am-4pm Sat
No Plastic   No Alcohol

Plate Lunch/Saimin
✧

Jane's has the sort of frozen-in-time appearance that nouveau places attempt to emulate, albeit in a sanitized, sterile sort of way. Yep, this is Hawaii, circa 1959, complete with swivel stools, chocolate sodas, saimin, a rather crappy jukebox, and a large varnished sea turtle tacked to the wall. Take a seat in one of the ratty but comfy booths, order from the large, handwritten menu on the back wall, and before you know it you're halfway expecting to see a crowd of revelers sauntering by on Liliha Street, celebrating the announcement of statehood.

No doubt but that a trip to Jane's is more about atmosphere than exceptional food. The eats here are decent but not particularly inspired—hamburgers, deviled egg sandwiches, plate lunches. You'll do well with the fried rice, containing tasty bits of char siu and topped with a fried egg, or the filling wun tun min, which is a noodle soup similar to saimin but more interesting, thanks to the addition of chubby stuffed won tons and a few vegetables. ♠

"We are the knights of Camelot,
We eat ham and jam and Spam-a-lot."

From the film **Monty Python and the Holy Grail**

90

JAVA JAVA

760 Kapahulu Avenue
732-2670

No Plastic

KAPAHULU
8am-11pm Mon-Th
8am-12am Fri-Sat
10am-5pm Sun
No Alcohol

Coffeehouse

✧

The nationwide resurgence of the coffeehouse has by no means bypassed the Islands; of the several around Oahu, Java Java makes the most zealous attempt at recreating the folkie aura of coffeehouses past by incorporating quality brew with live music and poetry readings. The menu includes sandwiches (go for the garden burger), fancy Belgian waffles with strawberries, pate with French bread, tabouli, and soups. Prices are in the $4-$6 range; the caliber of the food is high, though the portions are often espresso-sized. Skip the bagels, which are an unreasonable $2 each, but give the cheesecake a try; biscotti and some above-average baked goods. Coffee is decent but, ironically, less interesting than the food.

Atmosphere here is pleasant, even interesting: small, marble-topped tables and some art photos, with the looming possibility of a tarot reading courtesy of Sarina (there's a fee involved). Java Java also offers excellent potential for posing and/or poser-watching, depending on your own inclinations in that area. There's music, poetry, performance art—something virtually every night, either in the main room or upstairs in the Lizard Loft, a sort of cozy living room. The talent level fluctuates tremendously and there's often a cover charge, so be ready. Checkers and cards are available on request. And while you're in the neighborhood, check out the thrift store a few blocks down—they have one of the finest collections around of antique aloha shirts, some fetching hundreds of dollars. (Note: The Java Java folks also run the much less interesting Coffee Connection in Waikiki's Royal Hawaiian Shopping Center.) ♠

In eating, a third of the stomach should be filled with food, a third with drink, and the rest left empty.
Author unknown, Talmud

JO-NI'S

1017-A Kapahulu Avenue	KAPAHULU
735-8575	
Makai Market	ALA MOANA CENTER
945-7733	
11am-2pm, 5pm-9pm Daily	(Ala Moana all day)
VISA, MC	No Alcohol

Filipino

✧

Despite the decidedly unauthentic environs of both locations—one's in a mall food court, and the other has the bright and sterile genericness of a frozen yogurt shop—Jo-ni's in fact serves Filipino food of unquestionable legitimacy. The menu is far more comprehensive at the Kapahulu eatery, something of a crash course in Filipino cuisine. It's divided into sections that at times seem rather random and not necessarily mutually exclusive, so read carefully. In any event, all the standards can be gotten here, things like chicken adobo and the tomato-based pork sari sari, as well as pancit (noodle dishes). The lumpia are good and only $1.50 for a small order, and the soups can be outstanding. Foremost among these is sinigang—it's made with tamarind, which lends a distinct, pleasant sourness that's a common element in Filipino dishes. Added to this are long beans, Asian okra, and either prawns, pork, beef, or bangus (milkfish), whichever you fancy. Also worth serious consideration is the bright, brothy concoction made with chicken and green papaya.

The $3 halo halo is fruitier than most and superb, and it's one of the few instances in which the Ala Moana outlet is on par with the Kapahulu location. Desserts otherwise run about a dollar and include ube (a purple yam) ice cream and flan, both good. ♠

I thought tamarinds were made to eat, but that was probably not the idea. I ate several, and it seemed that they were rather sour that year. They pursed up my lips, till they resembled the stem end of a tomato, and

I had to take my sustenance through a quill for twenty-four hours...I found, afterward, that only strangers eat tamarinds—but they only eat them once.

Mark Twain, Mark Twain in Hawaii
(1866)

KATS SUSHI

715 S. King Street   DOWNTOWN
526-1268   11am-2pm, 5pm-10pm Mon-Fri
                    5pm-10pm Sat
VISA, MC   Bring Your Own

Sushi
✧

Fact: Even in America's most Japanized city, sushi costs big money. Sure, you can find it all over town—in fast food shops, on 7-11 counters, even in some vending machines—but the good stuff is pricey, particularly the style known as nigiri, or finger sushi (fresh seafood draped on a pad of seasoned rice). If you want decent sushi with zero fanfare for minimum bucks, Kozo Sushi is your spot. However, if you appreciate the aesthetics of a full-on sushi experience, complete with wisecracking fishmasters, wooden sashimi boards, good green tea in cool handleless mugs, and the chance to sample about 20 kinds of sushi (in unlimited quantities, mind you), Kats is the name to know. The price for all-you-can-eat is $16.95 at lunch, $18.95 at dinner. Though admittedly outside the realm of conventional bargain chowing, by sushi standards it's akin to a giveaway.

While other all-you-can-eat places come and go, Kat's has been in business for a decade, relying on superior product and word-of-mouth to attract customers. Most nights it's full right along until closing. The place itself is tiny, with maybe six tables and eight counter seats—sit here if possible so you can chat with the chefs and watch them work. Be advised, though, that they'll load you up with sushi just as fast as you can power it down, so take your time. Kats can be difficult to find and the location seems an unlikely one;

at night, they appear to be the only tenant in an unremarkable office building. The restaurant's interior is marked by sushi charts, a back wall filled with premium liquors parked there by regular customers, and a couple of sushi clocks—so if someone asks you the time and it happens to be, say, 8:30, you can wittily reply, "It's half past tako (octopus)." Try it on your next blind date. Trust me.

The food here is uniformly excellent, so pace yourself and try everything. The chefs, one of whom is the owner, tend to respond more readily to orders in garbled Japanese than flawless English, so check the chart in front of you. Be sure and try the abalone if they have it, the salmon, the ahi, the giant clam. Items like the sea urchin and the dark, musty mackerel aren't for everybody, and California rolls are the mayonnaisey variety, so be prudent. The rice rule is in effect here, which means you have to eat everything you order, otherwise they'll want to charge you a la carte prices and things can get ugly. Just don't get carried away, and make sure you're into sushi before you come. ♠

Then a roadsign:
  SWAMP GUINEA'S FISH LODGE
      ALL YOU CAN EAT!
An arrow pointed down a county highway. I would gorge myself. A record would be set. They'd ask me to leave. An embarassment to all.
          William Least Heat Moon, Blue
          Highways (1982)

KEVIN'S DRIVE-IN

100 N. Beretania Street   CHINATOWN
521-3439   7am-8pm Daily ("Monday to Sunday")
No Plastic   No Alcohol

Cantonese/Plate Lunch
◇

An often confusing aspect of the Hawaii dining scene is the way Asian restaurateurs take a peculiar license when co-opting American terms like *drive-in*. The irony here is that Kevin's is on a pedestrian mall, accessible only on foot. The area is Chinatown at its mellowest, with locals gathering not far from Kevin's door, suffusing the air with the clacking of mahjongg tiles and the animated hum of multilingual conversation—all day, every day.

These folks, in fact, represent Kevin's primary customer base. While you wait for your order, a steady stream of diminutive gentlemen step in, fishing in their pockets for coffee money. And in consideration of the modest means of the neighborhood clientele, Kevin's prices are among the cheapest around and portions are usually quite generous. Offerings include plate lunch faves (all $4 or less) like chicken katsu, loco moco, and sweet-and-sour spare ribs. As a general rule, the Chinese section of the menu holds the greatest rewards. They have the cheapest salt and pepper shrimp in the city ($4.35), tasty oyster chicken, and a tender and lemony chun pi duck, often described by the mild-mannered, bespectacled proprietress thusly: "Itsa steamed; itsa soft; itsa good."

Sandwiches are also worth a look here, and they tend in the direction of massiveness. Though hamburgers are under a buck, you're better off splurging on either the mahi sandwich or the chicken katsu sandwich (both $1.55), which isn't listed on the take-out menu. It's at least two thick inches of fresh-fried cutlet threatening to overwhelm the confines of the bun. Not a sandwich to be nibbled delicately, it must be dealt with on its own raucous terms, so find some napkins or take off your shirt. Kevin's interior is textbook Chinatown decrepit: four tables, a worn faux parquet floor, and a closet-sized kitchen that you probably don't want to investigate too closely. ♠

If it is fish you are looking for, why climb trees?
Chinese proverb

KIM CHEE

3569 Waialae Avenue	KAIMUKI
737-0006/737-6059	
46-010 Kam Highway	KANEOHE
235-5560	
1040 S. King Street	PAWAA
536-1426	

16 Kainehe Street   KAILUA
262-8888
98-150 Kaonohi Street   AIEA
487-2905
10:30am-9pm Daily   (hours vary)
No Plastic   Bring Your Own

Korean
✧

Though they are by no means identical, these places are owned by the same family, and all offer decent if not genius-quality Korean repasts for better than average prices. The Kaimuki location is especially popular—a fact not always readily apparent since, like many of the other restaurants along this stretch of Waialae Avenue, they tend to keep their drapes drawn during business hours.

Once inside the inner sanctum, you'll find a menu that sticks pretty tightly to Korean standards—dishes like bi bim bap, chop chae (a pan-fried combo of rice and long rice noodles, with assorted bits of vegetable and meat), and the requisite barbecued meats, of which beef's the one to get. These all run in the $4.50-$6.50 range, and for a buck or two more you can foray into the seafood realm, where you'll find good bets like pan-fried squid with hot sauce. There's also a variety of deep-fried and pan-fried fish, but keep in mind that Koreans like their fish to taste pretty fishy, so order accordingly. All meals are served with seaweed soup, excellent kim chee, and assorted other marinated vegetables of moderate quality.

The atmosphere here is agreeable enough in a synthetic sort of way, and the red vinyl, three-quarter wraparound booths are about the best you'll find anywhere. They fit nicely in a setting otherwise distinguished by bad Muzak (yeah, yeah, an oxymoron) and a stunning assortment of flowers and plants, all of which are fake. ♠

50 years hence...we shall escape the absurdity of growing a whole chicken in order to eat the breast or wing, by growing these parts separately under a suitable medium.

Winston Churchill, "50 Years Hence," *Popular Mechanics* (1932)

KIN WAH CHOP SUEY

45-588 Kam Highway   KANEOHE
247-4812/247-5024   10am-9pm Daily
VISA, MC   Alcohol Served

Cantonese

    Kin Wah enjoys a rather lofty reputation on the Windward side, due in no small part to their proven ability to serve up great sizzling platters, fine char siu, and daily specials which are unusual, delicious, and, especially in the case of seafood, extremely affordable. For the most part portions are adequate but not huge, so consider kicking off with some soup. Though they offer perhaps the cheapest bird nest ($7.50) and shark fin ($15) you're likely to find, go instead with the $5 combination soup, a hearty conglomeration of pork, duck, squid, chicken, long rice, and won bok.

    Be sure and scan the tiny Bud sign over the bar that lists daily specials. Expect to find the likes of clams with black bean sauce, poached prawns, beef with asparagus, sweet-and-sour fish fillet, and fried taro duck. These usually run in the $6 range, give or take. The much-ballyhooed sizzling platters are brought to your table as separates, then united amid a satisfying cloud of aromatic steam. Try the brick-red, slightly sweet Mongolian beef, or the combination seafood with vegetables, one of the more expensive items in the house at $6.50. A deft hand at the wok is revealed in vegetable dishes like mushrooms and vegetables with almonds or cashews. Celery, bamboo shoots, carrots, black mushrooms and the like are combined in a light sauce, each cooked enough to be hot but still in full possession of their respective textural integrities. Noodle fans should check out the ample crispy gau gee mein with chicken.

    Crowds are common at Kin Wah, the clientele diverse. The volume level approaches cacophony at times, what with families, ladies from the office, and blue-collar types taking a break to munch some char siu. The interior has booths and good-sized round tables, and decor consists primarily of an ornate ceiling and several large prints of carp. The parking situation can be vexing at peak times. ♠

A good breakfast is no substitute for a large dinner.
Chinese proverb

KOREAN BBQ CORNER

818 Iwilei Road   IWILEI
528-0311   6am-5pm Mon-Fri
                                               6am-3pm Sat
No Plastic   No Alcohol

Korean

✧

This cinder-block building is neighbor to Honolulu landmarks young and old—it sit's across from the new K-Mart (whose employees are forever drifting in for a quick bite), in the shadow of the giant pineapple at the Dole cannery. Though literally a shout away from Chinatown, Iwilei bears little if any of that neighborhood's decrepit charm. It's strictly warehouse territory, with little to recommend it aside from the monster Korean plates you'll find here.

$5 is the magic number at the BBQ Corner. That buys a plate heaped with rice, macaroni salad, assorted Korean-style vegetables, and flaming-hot kim chee counterbalanced by cool chunks of tofu. Selecting a single meat to round out this ensemble can be difficult, which is why the combination plates are the best way to go. Besides kal bi, bulgogi, and some very fine barbecue chicken, they offer a terrific fish jun, made with thin-sliced mahi dipped in an egg batter and fried when you order it. Also excellent is the hot spicy chicken, not so much fiery as it is insanely crisp. Delicious, that one. The fried squid is also a nice choice, and they offer a strong version of the Korean catchall bi bim bap as well as soups, including the seriously hot yook gae jang, chocked with vegetables, beef, long rice, and egg. It's the most expensive thing in the house at $5.95.

Whitewashed walls, a pocked concrete floor, the low hum of multiple A/C units, a dining area made up of assorted plastic patio furniture: this is the Korean BBQ Corner in all its decorative splendor, and you'll either love it or hate it—in which case you should opt for takeout. Besides Korean food, they also do a steady business in both cigarettes and hamburgers, which are large and cheap and highly regarded in the neighborhood. Posted about the premises are signs reading "No Smoking After Breakfast." ♠

We are indeed much more than we eat, but what we eat can nevertheless help us to be much more than what we are.

Adelle Davis, Let's Get Well (1965)

KOZO SUSHI

2334 S. King Street	MOILIILI
973-5666	
900 Fort Street Mall	DOWNTOWN
522-9517	
99-115 Aiea Heights Drive	AIEA
483-6800	
1150 Bishop Street	DOWNTOWN
522-9515	
4618 Kilauea Avenue	KAHALA
733-5733	
98-1005 Moanalua Road	AIEA
483-6805	
711 Keeaumoku Street	PAWAA
944-8881	
Koko Marina Shopping Center	HAWAII KAI
396-8881	
Windward City Shopping Center	KANEOHE
235-8881	
9am-7pm Mon-Sat	9am-6pm Sun (hours may vary)
No Plastic	No Alcohol

Sushi
✧

This is *the* place to go if you want some really decent sushi for rock-bottom prices. It's pretty much all takeout, and they do both single meals and large party trays. Most of the items here are quite good (and according to their sign, "guaranteed for two hours from time of purchase"), but for these prices you can forget about the fanfare that usually accompanies this trendiest of foods. The setting is defined by white tile floors, plastic trays, canned oolong tea, and soy sauce in plastic fish-shaped vials. Decoration consists of little more than a few signs explaining the recent switch to a different brand of rice and requesting that you speak up if you prefer your sushi without wasabi, the sinus-searing horseradish mustard.

Kozo cranks out maki sushi (hand rolls wrapped in seaweed) of all types—crab and cucumber, squid, shrimp, salmon, egg, ume (a dried plum), Spam—most any of which cost about a dollar each. They also have the fancier nigiri sushi, made with much larger portions of seafood and served with pickled ginger and wasabi. Six- to 15-piece meals run about $3-$5, which, in case you need to be told, is damn cheap. The menu's a little hard to understand, but like any self—respecting Japanese eatery they have a wonderful selection of plastic sushis, so you can just point to whatever looks good. They also sell green tea and miso soup. ♠

Rather cold tea and cold rice than cold words and cold looks.

Japanese proverb

KRISHNA KITCHEN

51 Coelho Way   NUUANU
593-4913   11am-2pm, 5pm-8:30pm Mon-Sat
                        4:30pm-6:30pm Sun (Transcendental Love Feast)
No Plastic   No Alcohol

Vegetarian/Indian
✧

Understand this about Hare Krishnas: Aside from being perfectly tireless chanters, they're pretty darn handy in the kitchen. They're also devout vegetarians, and with meat-free eateries being about as common in Hawaii as hog-calling contests and guys named Sven, Krishna Kitchen is a welcome oasis for flesh-avoiders. Here they can sup with confidence, never having to inquire whether a dish contains oyster sauce or chicken stock; and everything containing dairy products is labeled as such.

This is a buffet arrangement, and it's located in the International Society for Krishna Consciousness—actually an immense, elegant house in a residential neighborhood, so when you think you've come to the wrong place, you're there. The interior is serene, with wood paneling and plenty of plants; omnipresent is the heavy odor of incense. You'll see devotees drifting by in flowing garb, bidding you good day, but you won't be witnessed to or otherwise hassled. This a *very* low-key restaurant, not a recruiting office, and fears of jaunting in with an appetite and wandering out with a glazed look and a funny haircut are simply unfounded.

Cost is $6.50 at lunch and $7.50 at dinner, when there's always a hot entree. Various ethnic styles are alternated—Mexican, Italian, Chinese, with Indian popping up about every other night—so you may find vegetable pakoras or maybe eggplant parmigiana. Though macrobiotic simplicity is the operative concept here, they're not averse to spices, as their fine tomato sauces attest. Stir-frys and curries are customary, and there's almost always terrific dal, redolent of coriander and mustard seed. The lemon rice with cashews is fragrant and delicious. Rather surprisingly, their tortilla chips compare favorably with any in town—sturdy and unsalted, not greasy in the least; unfortunately, the salsa falls far short of the ideal. Whole wheat bread is homemade and consistently terrific. Salad bar items are simple but always fresh, and a couple of the  dressings, the miso-ginger and the smooth and nutty almond, are especially memorable. Also excellent are the non-dairy cookies.

If you desire a more immersionary Krishna experience, check out the Transcendental Love Feast on Sundays. It features a complete Indian meal and group chanting, all for the cost of a bad mai tai in Waikiki. Wear loose clothing and come hungry. ♠

Cooking is one of those arts which most require to be done by persons of a religious nature.
Alfred North Whitehead

KUA AINA SANDWICH

66-214 Kam Highway	HALEIWA/NORTH SHORE
637-6067	11am-8pm Daily
No Plastic	Bring Your Own

Sandwiches/Burgers
✧

In Hawaiian, kua aina means the country, countrified, rustic, rural. When surf's up, the line of traffic on Kam Highway may make you think of H-1 at rush hour, but Haleiwa town remains a

sylvan territory, and Kua Aina is North Shore grinds at their pin-
nacle. Like many a fine eatery before them, Kua Aina concentrates
on a single area of expertise, with uniformly satisfying results.
Burgers here are hefty things, with a half-pounder costing a shade
under $5. They're made with Manoa lettuce, tomato, grilled onions
and a splash of vermouth—real works of art, these. Options include
bacon, five kinds of cheese, pineapple, and mild green salsa. The
folks here aim for quality, so it may take a bit longer than at burger
palaces we can all name. They're well worth the wait.

Besides burgers, Kua Aina also offers up some truly righteous
sandwiches, most notably a grilled mahi version. This mild, white
fish is an Island mainstay, and no one serves it between the slices
any better than Kua Aina. Swabbed with their homemade tartar
sauce it's fine, very fine. Other options include teriyaki chicken,
thin-sliced roast beef, and a righteous BLT with avocado. In fact, if
you like avocado at all, get it here: for only a few cents extra they
load you up with half a unit. Messy, but delicious. The julienne fries
are superb—delicate and crispy, with a large order ($1.50) enough
for two to share.

The shop's small interior has plenty of wood: floors, tables,
paneling. Its usually busy, with a fairly diverse crowd. The walls
are covered with cool pictures of old Haleiwa, including the regal
Haleiwa Hotel. There are also plenty of shots of various death-
cheaters plying their craft: surfing, hang gliding, skydiving, even a
guy *bodysurfing* in 15-foot swells. ♠

---

*A man hath no better thing under the sun, than to
eat, and to drink, and to be merry.*
Ecclesiastes 8:15

KWONG ON CHINESE MERCHANDISE

3620-A Waialae Avenue KAIMUKI
734-4666 7:30am-3pm Mon-Sat
No Plastic No Alcohol

Manapua
✧

Some folks claim Kaimuki is Honolulu's last real neighborhood. It has schools, banks, a key shop, a taxi stand, a bewildering
number of beauty shops, a couple of bakeries, an 18-seat movie
theater with reclining chairs, a plethora of good restaurants, a night

club or two, and no high-rises. As befits the surroundings, Kwong On is small and puts on no airs, and it's hardly the sort to advertise. Their sign, in fact, is puny, and any view from the street is obstructed because they use the large front window for storing cases of soda, styrofoam takeout containers, and trays of boiled peanuts. So much for marketing.

Inside, one wall is devoted to items like oyster sauce, dried noodles, and quick-frying shrimp chips in assorted colors. It's takeout only, you'll soon discover; if there's a crowd, grab a number. Despite the smallness of the place, it often seems as if there are 20 people working here, so waits are usually brief.

Hot dishes are generally decent but unremarkable; however, you'll want to try the chow fun, embellished with plenty of cabbage, carrots, and bits of char siu. The primary items of interest, though, are the baked goods, most any of which will do you quite right, and they're as cheap as any around. The manapua, which come either steamed or baked, are modest in size but only 55 cents each. Get the baked curry chicken if they have them, and the curry half moons are also killer. On the sweet side, the 30-cent jin dui, with its slightly crunchy exterior and chewy coconut interior, is tough to beat at any price. Be advised that on most days all the baked items are gone by around 1 p.m. Kwong On also sells Chinese dried snacks like water chestnuts and lotus root. ♠

So long as there is bread to eat, water to drink and an arm to sleep on happiness is not impossible.
Chinese proverb

LA BAMBA

847 Kapahulu Avenue   KAPAHULU
737-1956   11am-2pm, 5pm-9:30pm Sun-Fri
No Plastic   Bring Your Own

Mexican
✧

The decor at La Bamba leans toward neo-taqueria, with faint overtones of junior high basement makeout settings, minus the beanbag chairs. Ten tables are jammed into a small trapezoid of a room, with prefab paneling, woven baskets on the wall, and a tile mosaic of a matador doing his thing. Remarkably, there's no Enormous Sombrero in view—but there can be a crowd. In the evenings,

103

a 15-minute wait is not uncommon.

La Bamba's menu is an above average lineup of the predictable suspects, with a few nice twists. The platos Mexicanos come with rice (dull) and beans (not bad), and a strong choice here is the Taco Mexico City. It has lean, shredded beef served with Maui onion and cilantro—ask for a wedge of lime and you're in business. The carne al carbon (grilled steak) tacos are also good, and the tamales come with a decent pork filling, though they lack some of the resiliency of the genuine article. Most of the standards fall in the $6.50-$8 range, while the more elaborate Mexican dinners hover around $10-$12. Best bets among the latter are the chicken cooked in green sauce, and the splendid chicken and beef fajitas. This is also one of the few places in all of Hawaii where you can get chicken in mole sauce. For dessert, the best move is to pay your tab and step lively down to Dave's for some of that wicked green tea ice cream. ♠

He who does not mind his belly will hardly mind anything else.
Samuel Johnson

LA GELATERIA

819 Cedar Street   PAWAA
591-1133   9am-5pm Mon-Fri
No Plastic   No Alcohol

Ice Cream

✧

Chances are good that if you fly first class to either Japan or the Philippines, you'll be eating Maurice Grasso's gelato. Of course, if that's how you travel it's not real likely you'll be reading this book— no matter, because Grasso's several dozen flavors are also available at his small but culinarily sophisticated operation here in town. Originally from Italy, Grasso achieved gelato Grand Master status in his homeland a few years back (yep, they have exams for these sorts of things), and his inspired frozen creations have won numerous awards since then.

When it comes to inventing flavors, Grasso has to be considered something of a genius. He's a tireless experimenter, and the extent to which he has mined the rich vein of local produce is unparalleled. We're not just talking passion fruit, mango, papaya— the man has made sherbets from such exotica as pikake (a fragrant

white flower often used in leis) and Surinam cherries (this he sometimes concocts for Roy's in Hawaii Kai). It's simply impossible to go
wrong here—for gelato, check out the
chocolate-passion fruit, the potent
espresso, or the refreshing white choco-
late-ginger, and sherbetwise, you've got
to try the lemon grass—and prices are
no more than at the supermarket.
A pint of sherbet is $3.25 with
gelato about 50 cents more; for
$1.30 you can get smaller cups
which are about the same size
as a hefty scoop. This is a modest operation, and when you
walk in you're practically stand-

ing in the main kitchen. Strike up a conversation with one of the
friendly workers, and you may get to taste whatever's being made
at the moment. A must visit. ♠

---

*Great Grandfather said, "In Hawaii the papayas are
so big, the children scoop out the seeds and carve faces
and light candles inside the shell. The candles grow on
trees. You can make black ink from the nuts of that
same tree.*

Maxine Hong Kingston, China Men
(1980)

LAPPERT'S ICE CREAM

2005 Kalia Road (Hilton Hawaiian Village)	WAIKIKI
943-0256	
Lower Level	ALA MOANA CENTER
942-0320	
7am-10pm Daily	(Ala Moana open mall hours)
VISA, MC, AMEX (Waikiki only)	No Alcohol

Ice Cream

If you've flown with Hawaiian Airlines, you've probably noticed Mr. Lappert's full-page ads in the inflight magazine. The story
goes that he came to Hawaii to enjoy retirement, only to end up
starting a successful ice cream venture on Kauai almost by accident.

To hear him tell it, at least, the guy just can't seem to help making money wherever he goes.

Mr. Lappert's horn-tooting notwithstanding, his operation turns out some pretty fair ice cream. And as designer brands continue to proliferate like fruit flies, Lappert's has, along with Dave's, put Hawaiian ice cream on the confectionary map. Much of the attraction here lies in their liberal use of local ingredients, which appeals not only to locals but also gives even the most cautious tourists a safe snatch of Island exotica. Lappert's uses Big Island coffee like there's no tomorrow, and the Kona Blue Espresso is the best thing going for an unadulterated java jolt in lickable format. Macadamia nuts also make frequent appearances, sinfully colluding with coffee, chocolate, coconut—whatevah.

Mainland traditionalists will find some solid options in the rum raisin and the touted cookies-and-cream. Sherbets also rate highly: the selection includes papaya, guava, mango and pineapple. All together there are around 40 flavors, and a single scoop (plain cones only, for some reason) runs $1.75, a double $2.80. There's usually a flavor of the day for about a buck a scoop. Steer clear of the shave ice unless desperate, as it's a pale imitation of the real McCoy. ♠

Every great feast has its last course.
Chinese proverb

LEE HO FOOK

100 N. Beretania Street	CHINATOWN
536-6077	10:30am-2:30pm, 5pm-8pm Wed-Mon
No Plastic	No Alcohol

Cantonese

✦

What we have here is basically a Cantonese eatery, pocket-version, lacking both the banquet facilities and 200-item menu common to many establishments. The scrunchy, six-table interior is characterized by sections of wallpaper used as artwork. Observe please the wall of stampeding white horses that give the unnerving sensation of having landed in a Marlboro ad—were it not, that is, for the bright orange "NO SMOKING" sign tastefully adhered to one stallion's rippling brisket. Another wall celebrates the pastoral life of the Old Country, complete with thatched huts and water buffalo in muted tones.

Oh yes...the food. The menu's heavy on soups and noodles, often in tandem. The won ton look fun is mild and satisfying, enhanced by a chile oil/shoyu/white pepper mixture of your own making. Another strong option in this department, not so commonly seen and something of a house specialty, is cake noodle. This is cooked lo mein that's then pan-fried and cut into squares; it's sensational and a very different trip texturally, what with the crispy edges. Try either the house special or meat combination versions, which seem remarkably similar (squid, shrimp, fish cake, char siu, vegetables) and run about $5 each.

Exceptional versions of cliched dishes are always a nice find, and Lee Ho Fook's big score is the sweet-and-sour pork ($5). It may well bring you back to the fold if you've become wearied by the excessive sweetness of most renditions. Get ready for a refreshing vinegar tang, a sauce that's closer to mustard-yellow than the usual strawberry-red glaze, and lean meat that's fresh-fried, with a crispy exterior devoid of breadiness. First class. ♠

Eating and mating are human instincts.
Meng Tzu, Book of Mencius

LEGEND SEAFOOD

100 N. Beretania Street	CHINATOWN
532-1868	10:30am-2pm, 5:30pm-10pm Mon-Fri
	8am-2pm, 5:30pm-10pm Sat-Sun
VISA, MC, AMEX	Alcohol Served

Dim Sum
✧

Though the sizable menu here is certainly worth your attention in its own right—featuring items like baked live crab with spicy salt and braised sea cucumber with shrimp roe—it's the dim sum that brings folks through the door in droves every day. The high-ceilinged dining room is huge, with very few of the tables designed to seat less than six people. Dumplings and the like are served until 2 p.m., and are somewhat pricier than at China House or Yong Sing. White tablecloths are everywhere, as is a staff of what seems like dozens, all roaming around taking orders or hawking goodies (many of

107

which aren't listed on the menu) from their carts. One side of the room is being dealt custard tarts, lotus seed buns, and sweet cream manapua; a few tables away, patrons are ogling roast duck stuffed with sweet soybeans, chicken in paper, black bean pork ribs, and a platterful of braised chicken feet; in still another area a waiter sidles by, his wagon jammed with bamboo steamer racks stacked six high and filled with manapua, shrimp dumplings, and shumai. Ordering can be rather hectic if you aren't fairly familiar with dim sum items, so you might as well live on the edge and simply go with whatever's offered by the suggestion-minded crew. Dim sum is perhaps best enjoyed in conjunction with other dishes, and Legend encourages this approach by backing their dumpling list with a noodle menu. These tend to be of impeccable freshness, and served in portions so gargantuan that small children may be frightened. The Legend pan-fried noodle with seafood ($7.95) is a particular standout, as is the stir-fried look fun with beef, featuring a mountain of pleasantly chewy wide noodles and stalks of the Chinese green of choice, choy sum. ♠

In my heart of hearts, of course, I have always believed that what may actually be my favorite dish in a number of Chinatown restaurants is something I have never even had the opportunity to taste, simply because of my inability to read the wall signs that announce some house specialties in Chinese.

Calvin Trillin, Alice, Let's Eat (1978)

LEONARD'S BAKERY

933 Kapahulu Avenue   KAPAHULU
737-5591   6am-9pm Sun-Th
                                        6am-10pm Fri-Sat

No Plastic   No Alcohol

Malasadas

✧

Although obscure on the Mainland, the round and yeasty Portuguese doughnuts known as malasadas are practically a staple in Hawaii. They're available at supermarkets, roadside stands and numerous bakeries, of which Leonard's is probably the most renowned.

Housed in a run-down, dingy building across from Crane Park,

108

Leonard's doesn't pretend to be anything it's not, and there's something of a time warp aura about the interior. Like any Portuguese bakery that takes itself seriously, they fry up malasadas continuously, so no matter when you drop by your order's always warm. Traditionally these airy orbs (cousins to the French beignet) are rolled in granulated sugar, but you can also get them plain. They cost 45 cents each, and a hungry man will usually start to balk by number four. They are slightly cheaper by the dozen, but be advised that they're meant to be eaten immediately and don't keep particularly well. Leonard's also offers pao doce, the Portuguese sweet bread, as well as a number of pastries and cakes. The chocolate doughnuts are worthwhile as are a number of other items, depending on your ability to withstand tooth-numbing sweetness. ♠

Sixty runners will not overtake him who breakfasts early.

Author unknown, Talmud: Baba Kamma

LIKE LIKE DRIVE INN

735 Keeaumoku Street
941-2515
No Plastic

ALA MOANA
24 Hours
No Alcohol

Coffee Shop
✦

At first blush this may seem like the sort of all-night coffee shop you find most anywhere in America: vinyl booths, a sizable smoking section, a Rockola jukebox, plenty of counter stools, burgundy carpet, and a staff of seen-it-all-before waitresses clad in sensible shoes and doubleknit uniforms. With a quick scanning of the menu, though, it quickly becomes apparent that you're most definitely not in Kansas anymore. The building looks like a bank, or the sort of place where you might store either hazardous substances or hazardous people.

Besides offering pretty standard breakfast fare, they serve up all manner of sandwiches—egg, Spam, Denver, burgers—and a fair selection of hot entrees. They stay busy throughout the day, and things can get especially crowded between 5:30 and 9 p.m., when they offer complete dinners that include soup, salad, entree, bread, beverage, and dessert for $6.50-$9. Main courses are usually rib-sticking affairs like pot roast with gravy, fried chicken, pork chops with fried bananas, spaghetti, shrimp tempura, and Ox Joint Jardi-niere—"If you have to ask what it is," cautions one waitress, "you probably don't need to be ordering it." After 9 p.m., you can get a pretty fair shrimp curry, cooked to order. The mondo fruit salad is nice, and house specialties like chili and rice, fried rice topped with fried eggs, and saimin are all above average. Otherwise, quality tends to vary widely here, which comes as no surprise when you consider that they make many items themselves and yet proudly advertise the fact that they serve Campbell soups. Desserts such as custard or banana pie are good and reasonably priced. ♠

You need not rest your reputation on the dinners you give.

Henry David Thoreau, Walden

LION COFFEE

831 Queen Street   KAKAAKO
521-3479   7:30am-5pm Mon-Fri
                                      8:30am-3pm Sat
VISA, MC   No Alcohol

Coffeehouse

✧

    If you've spent more than half an hour in Hawaii, you've prob-ably heard of Lion Coffee. This stuff is everywhere, but not always brewed with the necessary reverence. To find it at its purest (and cheapest), you need to head for the source, which in this case is the factory store in lovely Kakaako. Here, amid the auto-industrial clamor of fender works, upholstery shops, and tire recappers, is where the giant of the Hawaii coffee industry roasts and packages its beans. And this is also where you'll find, with the not-so-distant whir of pneumatic tools reverberating in your ears, the best coffee bargain in the Islands.

    They have bagels and assorted danishes and muffins here, which, though decent, are nothing special. Coffee is the raison d'etre, and Lion offers it in eight flavors. The Kona blends are all exceptional, as are the mac nut-flavored brews. Prices are tough to beat—a 12-ounce cup is 75 cents with refills a quarter, and a 20-ouncer runs all of a buck. Better still, espresso is $1, cappuccino $1.25, and a 20-ounce latte is $1.50—cheapest anywhere this side of Seattle. Lion also serves Thai coffee made with sweetened condensed milk, and a ridiculously rich mocha version made with Ghirardelli chocolate. Everything's available regular or decaf, iced or hot, with whole milk or skim.

Quite unsurprisingly, the interior reeks of java, and it's stocked with bagged coffee as well as all manner of related paraphernalia. There are a few seats inside and also a nifty covered patio, with a couple of Depression-era cookstoves used as counter space and a mini-library of cartoon books in the *Bloom County/The Far Side* vein. The staff is amiable and engaging, and a tour of the premises is yours for the asking. ♠

I have measured out my life with coffee spoons.
T.S. Eliot

LUNG FUNG

Niu Valley Shopping Center
377-5555/377-5566
VISA, MC, AMEX

NIU VALLEY
11am-9pm Daily
Alcohol Served

Cantonese

If you're feeling flush, there are impressive meals to be had in this area (try the Swiss Inn next door, or head to the much-acclaimed Roy's, just down the line toward Hanauma Bay). For memorable cheap eating, though, Lung Fung is pretty much it between Kahala and Waimanalo—unless you count the free samples at Costco in Hawaii Kai. Housed in a shopping complex of late-60's vintage, Lung Fung is roomy inside, the sort of place that attracts families and large groups. All the waitresses wear matching red tops, and they know their stuff.

Lung is the most powerful species of dragon according to Chinese lore, and Fung is the phoenix; together they represent good luck, which you shouldn't have to rely on to dine well here, provided you follow a few suggestions. As is typical with Cantonese eateries, the menu is extensive; as a general rule, you should pay closest attention to the first items listed in each section. For example, Lung Fung's Famous Lemon Chicken is exquisite—boneless, crispy-fried, coated but not smothered in a light and tangy sauce, topped with sliced lemons. They also do a nice job with the sweet-and-sour concept, with both the pork and the shrimp Canton coming up very strong. Though the roast duck is celebrated, go instead with the deep-fried, boneless pressed duck, meant to be slathered in plum sauce and downed with sweet steamed buns (these look like flattened manapua, and an order of eight is about $4). The first-is-best rule fails when it comes to noodles; though they sound quite appetizing, they aren't up to the caliber of other dishes and are best avoided, as is the char siu. Vegetarian options are few and far between, prices run mostly in the $5-$8 range, and portions are generous. ♠

Though there are a hundred ways to cook rice, there are only three religions.
Chinese proverb

MABUHAY CAFE

1049 River Street
545-1956
VISA, MC

CHINATOWN
10am-10pm Daily
Alcohol Served

Filipino
✧

Mabuhay has been around for 30 years, most of it spent in a ratty little space just around the corner from their present location. Truth be told, the new place looks respectable enough to make you worry, what with it's bright, tidy interior and checked tablecloths. But the thrift store art, bizarre jukebox, and pictures of the proprietors shaking hands with a puckered Ferdinand Marcos provide ample reassurance that things are basically as they've always been.

Simply put, this is the finest Filipino restaurant in the Islands, and also one of the best dining values (all dishes are in the $5-$8 range, most around $6). Meals here are enormous, due in part to the monstrous servings of rice—as one Filipino diner explains it, "most Filipino food is simply an excuse to eat rice." The dishes themselves are also quite large, though, centering mostly around chicken, pork, or seafood, primarily fish and shrimp. Offerings to watch for are the chicken adobo, cooked until tender in a dark gravy, and the chicken with marrongay (horseradish) leaves, which resemble hedge clippings but lend a wonderful, subtle flavor. Pork gisantes, a traditional favorite made with green peas and tomatoes, is terrific, as is the tomato-based shrimp sarciado (also available with chicken). The peanut-based stew, kare kare, is available here, and the noodle dishes are superior to any around. If you're Filipino or share their passion for things intestinal, you'll find those items as well.

Desserts include the national favorite halo-halo, which contains chipped ice, milk, chewy palm fruits, purple yam, and other knick knacks. Served in a tall glass, it's meant to be mixed, and Mabuhay's is quite sweet. They also have ice creams made from the aforementioned yam (ube), as well as other flavors—mango, jackfruit—which are quite good and unlike anything you'll likely find at Baskin-Robbins. ♠

The appetite is sharpened by the first bites.
Jose Rizal

MAI LAN

1224 Keeaumoku Street   MAKIKI
955-0446   10am-9pm Tue-Sun
VISA, MC   Bring Your Own

Vietnamese

In Honolulu's continually expanding throng of Vietnamese eateries, Mai Lan stands as something of an elder statesman, having been in business for nearly a decade and a half. During that span, they've seen competitors come and go, yet they've remained steadfast. And though the food isn't superlative nor the prices the cheapest, they can be counted on for consistently fine meals and gracious service. Mai Lan does little beyond a small sign to beckon customers. The interior is stark but comfortable, with a few interesting artworks depicting raven-haired women playing traditional musical instruments.

Appetizers of note include the tightly wound shrimp rolls ($1.85 each) and light and luscious steamed dumplings. The pho here is nothing special, but a number of the other soups ($6 or so) are well worth your attention. They are all variations on the same broth-and-noodles theme, with goodies like duck, shrimp cake, crab, chicken, and mustard cabbage standing in for beef. As with pho, the situation is brightened immeasurably by aromatic herbs, cool sprouts, and a shot of lime. Most interesting of the plates is the thick noodles with pork sausage and vegetables; definitely tasty, but texturewise it's not for everyone. Lovers of some serious fire will be made giddy by the container of pickled red and green chiles with garlic, the armchair equivalent of a trip to the sweat lodge. The iced coffee with condensed milk is excellent—they use the chicory-laced blend sold by New Orleans's Cafe du Monde, though they don't like to admit it—and the sweet, salty li hing mui beverage is good as well. Desserts include the sensually arresting sung sa hot lu, chocked with coconut milk, agar agar (gelatin made from seaweed) and bright red pomegranate tapioca. ♠

The spirit cannot endure the body when overfed, but, if underfed, the body cannot endure the spirit.
Saint Frances de Sales

MAI'S DELI

1501 Kapiolani Boulevard   ALA MOANA
955-6583   10am-6pm Mon-Sat
No Plastic   No Alcohol

Vietnamese

This is an A-1 example of a place that's not at all as it appears. Apparently Mai's was in an earlier incarnation a fast food joint of meager dimensions, and the plastic seats and tables are bolted to the floor. But if the looks suggest eats no more compelling than those found at your finer theme parks, even a cursory gander at the menu says think again. You'll discover this is actually a stellar Vietnamese eatery with a chowlist as eclectic as any in the city, and that includes Chinatown, though there never seems to be anybody dining here.

Besides serving up spring, summer, autumn, and winter rolls, each with their own dipping sauce, Mai's has absolutely wondrous sandwiches, served on French rolls. These run from $2.50-$3.50. Order either the meatless or shredded pork chop version—the latter adorned with roasted rice, garlic, and goosed with a few shots of fish sauce.

Mai's bo tai ($4.95) is a must—a salad of thin-sliced beef, garlic, onion, mint, cilantro, lemon juice and crushed peanuts, it embodies everything sexy about Vietnamese food. Pho takes a back seat here to an impressive array of soups and Chinese-inspired noodle dishes, some of them rarely if ever found elsewhere in Hawaii. Try any or all of the crispy noodle dishes—delicate, faintly sweet, and delicious—or crab meat and rice noodle soup, with eggs, parsley and mint in a broth. Wow. Or perhaps you'll bun mang vit, made with duck, bamboo shoots, herbs, lemon and made tomato fancy the dried pepper. Whatever you decide on, prices are all in the $4.50-$6 bracket; just do what feels good and let the devil take the hindmost.

The mood here is relaxed and the English speaking minimal, so it's not inconceivable that they'll forget part of your order, which they rarely bother to commit to paper. The food arrives quickly from the kitchen, which, as with most Vietnamese joints, is an insanely cramped corner filled with steaming pots, toppled fish sauce containers and stray utensils. As per usual, the iced coffee with condensed milk—like many a seemingly simple Vietnamese delight, deceptively difficult to recreate in the home—is beyond reproach and sells for $1.75. Even the ice is perfect. ♠

One laughs when joyous, sulks when angry, is at peace with the world when the stomach is satisfied with food.

Hawaiian proverb

THE MANAPUA SHOP

1104 Bishop Street   DOWNTOWN
521-3288   6am-5pm Mon-Fri
         7:30am-2pm Sat
No Plastic   No Alcohol

Manapua

✧

While capitulating to the neon look of its neighbors—this is downtown, after all, and the tendency is to cater to the upwardly-mobile, button-down crowd—the Manapua Shop is essentially a Chinatown bao house dressed up for Bishop Street. Manapua and noodles are the options, and though the prices are slightly inflated thanks to the address, the food is quite good.

The 77-cent manapua are available steamed or baked, and either way they're fresh, warm, and amply endowed with quality ingredients. Besides the mandatory char siu (saucier and sweeter than Char Hung Sut's), the Manapua Shop stuffs their buns with things like crab, dry curry beef, and chicken. They also have a peppery vegetarian version as well as siapao, an item rarely seen in these parts and virtually unheard of on the Mainland. It's essentially a Filipino version of the manapua ($1.30) filled with salted duck egg, pork and spices, and it's definitely worth getting. Chow fun dishes are also tasty, and everything's for takeout only. ♠

Rely on Heaven for your meals.
Chinese proverb

MANOA HEALTH MARKET (ANDY'S)

2904 E. Manoa Road   MANOA
988-6161   7am-6pm Sun-Fri
VISA, MC   No Alcohol

Smoothies/Sandwiches

Manoa residents are well aware of the lunch and breakfast bargains to be had at Andy's, makers of one of Oahu's best smoothies. They manage to offer killer deals like a stack of banana pancakes for $2.50 by minimizing overhead expenses such as...well, square footage. Andy's is about as narrow as a restaurant can get without being referred to as a hallway, but there are a few miniature tables if you insist on eating here. Besides the bargain breakfasts, Andy's offers baked goods—chocolate or orange-mango muffins, raspberry bars, raisin-studded energy bars—which are ample, inexpensive, and generally excellent. The sandwiches are also a square deal and made fresh; they do a fine tuna melt, and expect anything involving cheese and avocado to be done well. Tread lightly in the area of Mexican items, such as the burritos, as this is clearly not their forte.

Hands down the best reason for heading to Andy's are the smoothies, though, made fresh with papaya, banana, strawberries, yogurt, coconut cream, lemonade, orange juice—what- ever you want. They are substantial, they are cheap (around $2), they are superb (just steer clear of the ones made with apple or grape juice). In addition to the above, Andy's sells pro- duce and car- ries a nominal selection of grocery items, along with a host of vitamins and dubious health aids which by all appearances are considerably less of a deal than the smoothies. ♠

If your eyes are set wide apart you should be a veg-etarian, because you inherit the digestive characteristics of bovine and equine ancestry.

Dr. Linard Williams (medical officer to the Insurance Institute of London) (1932)

MAPLE GARDEN

909 Isenberg Street   MOILIILI
941-6641   11am-2pm, 5:30pm-10pm Daily
VISA, MC, AMEX   Alcohol Served

Mandarin/Szechuan

According to their jovial menu, "each succulent morsel of every Szechuan course at Maple Garden stimulates a taste for more!" Never mind that the sign out front advertises *Mandarin* cuisine—in this Cantonese-dominated city, Northern and Western Chinese cooking styles have been hybridized, and Maple Garden's menu is a clear example of just how happy a marriage it can be.

A number of soups are offered, and the hot and sour (listed as "Sour Hot") is vaunted by the staff; skip it, and instead think about ordering an extra entree. Seafood's usually a reliable choice, and oft-mangled Northern standards like sauteed shrimp with cashews are here supplied with the proper voltage. The smoky Szechuan chicken is fabulous: light, crispy skin and meat that's juicy and smoke-permeated. It's chopped into manageable pieces and served with steamed rolls made from sweet dough. The spicy eggplant in garlic sauce is their most famous dish, and justifiably so. Maple Garden's version of this Honolulu mainstay has skinned eggplant sliced lengthwise and cooked soft, with plenty of ginger and more sweetness than heat. The popular Chinaman's Hat is a confluence of minced meat and vegetables, and it's served with thin pancakes in the mu shu pork style—about as unadulterated a Mandarin item as you're likely to find in these parts. Because vegetable dishes like the Grandma's tofu and the aforementioned eggplant are usually made with meat stocks, oyster sauce, or some other flesh-derived ingredient, the menu advises vegetarians to "please check with your waiter." Most dishes, meaty or no, run in the $6-$8 range.

Maple Garden has been serving spicy alternatives to Cantonese mildness for nearly 20 years, and the Wall of Fame bears testimony to visits by such luminaries as Sly Stallone, Barry Manilow and Johnny Mathis. The interior is quite nice, with large murals and prints, most featuring a goodly number of horses and mountains. The paneling and carved partitions are downright elegant, with large burnished wood booths further enhancing the setting. Waiters are knowledgeable pros, decked out in red collarless shirts. ♠

Rice affected by the weather or turned a man must not eat, nor fish that is not sound, nor meat that is high. he must not eat anything discolored or that smells bad. He must not eat what is overcooked, nor what is undercooked, nor anything that is out of season. He must not eat what has been crookedly cut, nor any dish that lacks its proper seasoning. The meat that he eats must not be enough to make his breath smell of meat rather than of rice. As regards wine, no limit is laid down; but he must not be disorderly.

Confucius (born 551 B.C.), The Analects of Confucius

MASA AND JOYCE FISH MARKET

45-582 Kam Highway   KANEOHE
235-6129
Temple Valley Shopping Center   KANEOHE
239-6966
9am-6pm Mon-Sat   8:30am-5pm Sun
                         (Kam Highway closed Tue)
VISA, MC   No Alcohol

Sushi/Poke/Plate Lunch

✧

     Masa and Joyce Fish Market—often referred to simply as Masa's—manages to cover a lot of culinary ground in a fairly small area. As a seafood market, they offer dried fish (including some choice aku sticks), killer sashimi, and an impressive rotating assortment of poke. Besides making a fine clam version, they also like to mix ahi with limu (seaweed), kukui nut, or Hawaiian rock salt—the list of offerings is dictated mainly by freshness and availability. And prices are reasonable, usually about $6-$8 per pound ($2 worth usually makes a nice snack for one person).

     As a restaurant, Masa's serves up plate lunches loaded with teri beef and the like, and they also offer the far less common pasteles—pork and unripe banana, wrapped in banana leaf and steamed. If this sounds more Caribbean than Polynesian, it's because these were introduced to the Islands decades ago by Puerto Rican workers—whose contribution to Hawaiian cuisine, incidentally, is rather unsung. At $7.50, the pasteles plate runs a couple of bucks more than other items, and they're listed with the qualifier "when available"; if the opportunity presents itself, go for it. Sushi items are generally good, though beware the mayonnaise-laden California rolls. ♠

Eat of the fish belly and you will be satisfied.
Hawaiian proverb

MASAGO'S

85-915-A Farrington Highway   WAIANAE
696-7833   7am-3pm Tue-Sun
No Plastic   Bring Your Own

Hawaiian/Japanese

✧

Masago's is a three-dimensional embodiment of the word *unassuming* and all but invisible from the road, making it especially difficult for first-timers to find. Located in a small building adjacent to an auto parts store, their presence is announced only by a modest sign tacked to a wooden fence, which in turn constitutes one edge of a splendid little gravel courtyard. If at all possible, eat out here amid the plants and birds and the occasional kitten; Masago's interior is pretty dreary, not to mention a shade warm—perhaps because no matter where you sit you're never more than about eight feet from the stove.

The staff is cheerful, engaging, and prone to recommending the fried rice (good advice). The menu is divided into Hawaiian, Japanese, and American foods; as sayeth Meat Loaf, two out of three ain't bad. Hawaiian eats are a la carte but reasonable: the lau lau ($2.95) is exceptional but often unavailable; the lomi salmon is the largest anywhere, served in a soup bowl; even better is the rarely seen lomi aku, definitely worth ponying up $4.50. Their poi is also excellent, and portions are bountiful.

Japanese meals are served in a wooden tray and include rice, miso soup and pickled vegetables. The tempura's decent but not incredible; give serious thought instead to the chicken katsu, watercress pork, or the deep and terrific pork eggplant. $6 will cover you on any of these. Breakfast choices include omelettes and mac nut pancakes. Masago's is a must if you're on the Leeward side. ♠

Let us consider for a moment lunch in the country. I do not mean lunch in the open air, for it is obvious that there is no meal so heavenly as lunch thus eaten, and I have no time to dwell upon the obvious.

A.A. Milne

MASU'S MASSIVE PLATE LUNCH

1808 Liliha Street   LILIHA
524-4368   6:15am-3pm Mon-Sat
No Plastic   No Alcohol

Plate Lunch

✧

In a world where orange juice is touted for it's calcium content and nutrition is ever the hot topic, Masu's is about as retro as it gets. The unwritten credo of this place, now in its 20th year of service, is enough to make any card-carrying AMA member whiff a 3-foot putt: *The Less Food Groups, The Better.*

Masu's has received several Best Plate Lunch awards, and they have a sizable (pun intended) and loyal following. Much of their popularity stems from the daily specials, which are printed up a month in advance and illustrate convincingly the old saw, Hawaiians don't eat until they're full—they eat until they're tired.

Common to all the specials is enough meat to make *The Jungle* seem like a stroll in the garden, and a typical repast reads thusly: "Fried pork chop with tonkatsu sauce, charcoal-broiled top sirloin steak, fried shrimp tempura, baked Spam, Melveen's famous Tita-style Vienna sausage, and tuna-potato salad." That racket you'll be hearing is your aorta, bulging and bursting like a $5 retread. As for standard items, the mahi and the teriyaki chicken are fairly tasty, but beware the disturbingly thick hamburger steak—best considered not as sustenance but rather a cheap, organic alternative to elevator shoes.

Despite being more about quantity than quality, Masu's draws a crowd and often sells out before noon, so you may want to call to make reservations—not for a table, but for a meal. No joke. Not surprisingly, they attract more than their share of serious eaters, as well as tottering old ladies from the neighborhood, who can be seen looking up from meals they haven't a prayer of finishing to wave at friends passing on the sidewalk. And the interior, it's classic plate lunch: a smattering of veneered tables, ceiling fans, fatigued brown carpet, Levolors dusty and bent, street noise wafting through the open doors. You can count on hearing local music of one form or another, and autographed photos include Butch Helemano, pro wrestler Ripper Collins, and several leering, overripe politicians. Happy flossing. ♠

121

It is a fact that great eaters of flesh are in general more cruel and ferocious than other men.
Rousseau

M. MATSUMOTO STORE

66-087 Kam Highway   HALEIWA/NORTH SHORE
637-4827   8:30am-5:30pm Daily
VISA, MC   No Alcohol

Shave Ice
✧

Like a number of other foodstuffs with which Hawaii residents identify strongly—malasadas, lau lau, poi—a good shave ice isn't nearly as easy to find as one might hope or expect. The North Shore has traditionally been something of a Mecca for such things, and you can score one of these syrupy delights all up and down Kam Highway—most notably at Aoki's, Miura Shave Ice, and the best known of the lot, Matsumoto's.

Matsumoto's certainly has the sort of time-worn, tumbledown appearance that instills confidence in the adventuresome gas-tronome. The place has been around forever, and besides being readily known to every Oahu resident it's frequently mentioned in travel guides. Contrary to what you may read, however, they don't have the best shave ice on the island (that you'll find at Moiliili's Waiola Store), but they do pile 'em high and sell 'em cheap. For little more than busfare you get an enormous ball of slightly crunchy ice, perched in a paper cone. Syrup flavors are pretty standard—pineapple, lemon-lime, banana—with passion fruit easily the top choice.

For my money, at least, the gaudily colored syrups (pineapple, for example, is a shocking blue) are a tad sweet and tend to taste alike; others will vehemently argue to the contrary, however, so check it out and decide for yourself. Shave ice was introduced to the Islands by Japanese immigrants come to work in the sugar cane fields, and the optional sweet azuki beans are their legacy. These have a passing resemblance to black-eyed peas and sometimes require a little getting used to for Western palates unaccustomed to the Asian predilection for sweet beans. Beware the determined bees hanging around the benches out front. Matsumoto's also sells crack seed, and fresh-boiled peanuts will set you back 80 cents. The T-shirts are pretty slick, too, if you're doing the souvenir thing. ♠

What you have, eat.
Hawaiian proverb

MEG'S COUNTRY DRIVE INN

66-200 Kam Highway	HALEIWA/NORTH SHORE
637-9122	
743 Waikamilo Road	KALIHI
845-3943	
	7am-6pm Daily
No Plastic	No Alcohol

Plate Lunch

Meg's North Shore outlet sits in the thick of Haleiwa town, across from the shopping center. Things are usually hopping here, and when the surf swells so do the lines. It's takeout only, with all business conducted through a couple of those sliding glass windows that define this sort of place.

The possibilities at Meg's can be described as plate-lunch plus, with a menu more diverse and daring than the vast majority of local-food dispensaries. Auxiliary choices encompass smoothies made with fresh fruit ($2), oxtail soup, kimchee, miso soup, and sandwiches—including an 8-ounce burger for $3 and change. All of this isn't to say that Meg's doesn't take the plate lunch gig seriously—they advertise 20 different kinds, including all the usuals like mahi mahi, pork cutlet, teriyaki chicken. But overall, the best bets are the Korean plates, with either the barbecue beef or chicken a solid way to go. All meals can be had for a five spot or less.

Situated perilously close to Kam Highway, Meg's is often an excellent venue for watching the surf traffic rumble by: bleachy dudes driving smoky rustbuckets, locals in tricked-out pickups, and tourists in rented minivans, camcorders at the ready. The only seating is on the small gazebo-like patio. Otherwise, you're on your own—which ain't such a bad way to be in this part of the world. ♠

The hungry man does not hear.
Swahili proverb

MINI GARDEN

50 N. Hotel Street   CHINATOWN
538-1273   10:30am-2pm, 6pm-12am Daily
No Plastic   No Alcohol

Cantonese

Ever since the city made a concerted effort a few years back to eradicate vice in Chinatown, the neighborhood's been relatively tame at night. Few restaurants around here are open late; Mini Garden's among the most nocturnal, and it's both a great place to eat and an excellent venue for watching the occasional dust-ups at the strip joints across the street.

Rather inocuous by day, Mini Garden is transformed when the sun fades. As the evening goes along, it becomes populated by an increasingly interesting stream of characters: noisy families; young Chinese professionals slurping noodles, talking on cellular phones and smoking like houses ablaze; elderly night-owls from the neighborhood, shuffling in for a bowl of the highly regarded beef brisket soup; couples whis-crispy gau gee. There's also a host of mysteri-ous characters from nearby Aala Park who drift in and out like wraiths, clutching small sacks and uttering nary a word. If you want to get a real sense of what Chinatown's like by night while dining well, have a seat.

The fare is basic Cantonese, neither ostentatious nor expensive. The stewed noodles with char siu is outstanding, as is for that matter anything with the lean and succulent sweet roast pork, as it's referred to on the menu. Soups also play big—noodles with roast duck, shrimp dumplings with noodle, won ton with duck feet—and they're terrific, across the board. Recommended offerings from the Special Dishes section include the Best Quality Roast Duck, and garden vegetables with oyster sauce; also listed here are shredded sea blubber and A Minute Boiled Pig's Liver, the quality of

124

which I'm afraid you'll have to determine for yourself. A nice pot of hot tea comes with the meal, and prices are so low ($4 buys any number of dishes) it almost feels like stealing. ♠

Young people relish fine clothes; old people prefer food.

Chinese proverb

MR. TURNER'S SOUTHERN CUISINE

30 Wilikina Drive
622-6996

No Plastic

WAHIAWA
5pm-8pm Tue-Fri
12pm-8pm Sat-Sun
No Alcohol

Soul Food
✧

Upon first glance it may seem rather odd that the only two soul food restaurants in Hawaii are half a block apart. But when you consider that soul food's as integral a part of the American black experience as soul music, and that Hawaii's largest concentration of blacks folks is across the road at Schofield Barracks, then the juxtaposition seems a little more sensible.

Unlike Teddy B's up the street, Mr. Turner's is takeout only, a situation obviated by the fact that his entire establishment, kitchen and all, is maybe 300 square feet. The interior is decorated with original artwork by Mr. T himself, who presides with authority over steam trays of authentic vittles. The posted menu can't always be trusted, but in general you can expect barbecue ribs, chitlins, and the like. Both the catfish and the smothered chicken are highly recommended, as are the black-eyed peas, slow-cooked with ham hocks. The most volatile offering is the red beans and rice with hot links. One bite and you'll know no punches have been pulled: these are smoky, fiery legumes, and the hefty sausage is neither oily nor devoid of red pepper in the least. In fact, all of the above are serious, take-no-prisoners soul food renditions—the sort of filling, calorie-laden chow to make Richard Simmons wake up screaming. Lean cuisine it ain't, so be ready.

Meals run $7-$8 and include rice, macaroni and cheese (nothing special), and cornbread—the cakey and faintly sweet yellow corn-meal variety that Southerners love to bash but the rest of America considers authentic. If greens are offered, by all means get 'em on

125

the side ($2). Ditto on the sweet potato pie, which is cheap ($1.50 slice/$8 whole pie) and absolutely prime—thin flaky crust, smooth filling that's not too sugary.

The building is whitewashed and pleasantly ramshackle, flanked by Mr. Soul Scissors on one side, KC's Barber, Style, and Shiatsu on the other. Mr. Turner takes seriously the old self-employment mantra about setting your own hours; times are posted, but it's altogether possible he'll be closed when the sign says open, and vice versa, so don't drive clear across the island without calling first. ♠

"How much are your yams?" I said, suddenly hungry.
"They ten cents and they sweet," he said, his voice quavering with age...I took a bite, finding it as sweet and hot as any I'd ever had, and was overcome with such a surge of homesickness that I turned away to keep my control.

Ralph Ellison, Invisible Man (1947)

H. MIURA STORE AND TAILOR SHOP

66-057 Kam Highway	HALEIWA/NORTH SHORE
637-4845	8am-5pm Mon-Sat
	10am-5pm Sun
VISA, MC, AMEX	No Alcohol

Shave Ice
✧

One of the cardinal rules for cheap eaters on the prowl is to go where the lines are; however, another rule is to never completely trust this first rule. It sometimes happens—I won't say often, but it does happen—that the most celebrated places are popular because of past reputation and are in fact not the best around. Exhibit A: Matsumoto's inarguably has the biggest rep of any shave ice spot in the galaxy, with lines snaking out the door, but their product isn't Haleiwa's best. That you'll find just down the street at the mom-and-pop Miura store, in business since 1918. Like most every other building in town, Miura is a simple and unassuming wooden structure with a metal roof, and it pretty well defines rural Hawaiian/ sugar plantation architecture. Even the nearby McDonald's has adopted the style.

Compared to both Matsumoto's and Aoki's, Miura isn't setting any sales records. But they deliver a fine, at times exceptional product. Though the ice texture suffers the same clumpiness as its competitors, some of the flavors here are, in my opinion, superior. By all means try the lilikoi, which may be the best version anywhere on the island—fragrant and pleasantly tart, it captures the essence of this sexy Isle fruit. Also, shell out the 20-cent premium for the coconut cream. More viscous and silky than syrups, it avoids excessive sweetness, greatly improves the texture of the ice, and is also downright delectable. In keeping with the neighbors, Miura serves up an almost unmanageably enormous shave ice for $1-$2 bucks, and the azuki beans are top-notch. ♠

I think that to get under the surface and really appreciate the beauty of any country, one has to go there poor.

Grace Moore, You're Only Human Once (1944)

MUI KWAI CHOP SUEY

45-1052 Kam Highway   KANEOHE
247-3230/247-5595   10:30am-9pm Daily
VISA, MC   Alcohol Served

Cantonese

✧

If when surveying the menu you experience a pang of deja vu, it may be because one of the cooks here decided to open his own place, Kin Wah Chop Suey, just up the road. The menus are nearly identical, which in the restaurant business can be taken as the sincerest form of flattery, but it's also a potential bore. Luckily, though, the deal turned out win-win, as Kin Wah has prospered and the departee's replacement clearly know's his or her stuff.

Though they have wonderfully cheerful waitresses and plenty of room to spread out (in huge construction-orange booths, no less), Mui Kwai sometimes appears to do more takeout business. Either way, the menu includes scads of seafood (try the shrimp fritters with vegetables for $6) and chow mein (go with the Mui Kwai chow mein or the cake noodles, both around $5). It may seem like every-

127

one here is eating the almond duck with sweet-and-sour sauce, and it's nothing short of fabulous. Just about any of the daily specials are to be embraced: look for items like sweet-and-sour fish fillet (they favor sea bass), clams in black bean sauce, beef with asparagus, or pork with choy sum—a Cantonese-favorite green otherwise known as swamp cabbage. Mui Kwai prepares it as well as anybody around. In fact, unlike some Chinese places they load on the vegetables here, and portions can be patently enormous, with one dish often enough to sate two moderate eaters. Vegetarians and other discriminating eaters are also in luck, as a number of vegetable, tofu, and noodle dishes are available sans MSG, salt, oil, and/or meat stock. All you have to do is give the word. ♠

Nearly everyone wants at least one outstanding meal a day.

Duncan Hines, Adventures in Good Eating (1936)

MY CANH

164 N. King Street   CHINATOWN
599-1866   8am-4pm Daily
VISA, MC   Bring Your Own

Vietnamese
✧

In recent years, the term Chinatown has become more and more of a misnomer. Though its complexion remains unmistakably Asian, an increasing number of non-Sino enterprises are slipping in amongst the herbalists, noodle factories and manapua shops. Vietnamese entrepreneurs have made the most significant inroads, operating a sizable number of restaurants and grocery stores. And seeing as Honolulu is North America's premier city in terms of Vietnamese food, it's no surprise that the overall level of Chinatown's Vietnamese eats is extremely high.

My Canh turns out great meals in the $5-$6 range, and as their menu explains, "Our talented chefs hold the beauty of presentation almost as high in his esteem as the taste." Uh-huh. Not surprisingly, most of the clientele is Southeast Asian, and lest you doubt My

Canh's sterling reputation among recent immigrants from the mother country, you need look no further than ...well, the sign above the commode, which reads, "Please Do Not Place Footwear on the Toilet Seat." Some items are listed only in Vietnamese. This is no great problem, however, as the walls are plastered with large photos of virtually every dish.

In addition to daily specials there are several appetizers, excellent shrimp rolls and the pricey-but-delicious sugar cane prawns (upwards of $8) among them. Soups here are delicious, and the pho is brilliant—even for ravenous eaters, the $5 Special Bowl can seem nigh on bottomless. The seafood soup is also highly recommended, as are the dry noodle dishes; be advised, however, that the rice dishes, as is often the case in Vietnamese eateries, are relatively bland and uninteresting. Captivating beverages include Soy Bean Drink, a cucumber-green elixir purported to be especially healthful. The mauve interior is cheery, bright and clean, with mirrors, a fish tank or two, small tables jammed with condiments, and a two-faced clock—one side reads "Vietnam," the other, "Local Time." ♠

Hawaii is probably the only state that ever entered the Union because of food.
Waverley Root and **Richard de Rochemont**, Eating in America (1976)

MYONG'S TAKE OUT

1505 Young Street
944-9075

No Plastic

PAWAA
9am-7pm Mon-Fri
9am-3pm Sat
No Alcohol

Korean
✧

This tiny Korean plate lunch joint sits across from the old police station, and until recently it was surrounded by the offices of enterprising bondsmen. But Honolulu's finest moved to fancier digs in the fall of 1992, and with them went the bail shops; Myong's has since expanded and thanks to the judicious purchase of some folding chairs, it is, strictly speaking, no longer just for takeout.

The menu's short and sweet, and virtually everything is reliable. Myong's demonstrates what something as simple as local-style plate lunch can become when put in the hands of skilled cooks. Besides rice, their plates features two kinds of kim chee—sesame sprouts and hot won bok—plus macaroni salad. With the exception of the beef jun, the meats—barbecue beef, kal bi, fried squid—are all of a high caliber, indeed. The barbecue chicken merits special mention, as it ranks with the best around: lean, skinless thigh meat, soaked in a gingery marinade and grilled. Superb. They also offer an interpretation of the Korean favorite bi bim bap, which they call bi bim rice; unlike most versions, it's meatless. Among the sandwiches, only the barbecue chicken is worthy of your attention.

Myong's is run by a middle-aged couple who remain amiable despite the tight confines of the place, which has an interior roughly equal in size to that of an early-70's Cadillac. Decor consists of two mammoth rice cookers, various and sundry refrigeration units, and a small TV usually tuned to Korean soap operas. Prices hover around $5, and portions are quite adequate. They don't sell beverages here, so you'll have to step outside to the vending machine. ♠

A man seldom thinks with more earnestness of any-thing than he does his dinner.
Samuel Johnson

NAYONG FILIPINO

2 N. Hotel Street
531-1846
No Plastic

CHINATOWN
10am-8:30pm Mon-Sat
No Alcohol

Filipino
✧

Nayong's modest quarters are crammed with tables and chairs, stacks of dishes, cassette tapes and mammoth rice cookers. There's also plenty in the way of plants, linoleum, and rattan, plus flowery orange and yellow wallpaper that looks like it came straight out of your spinster aunt's kitchen. The clientele, meanwhile, runs the Chinatown gamut: one minute it's tiny, gaunt-faced Filipino men who grew up around here, the next it's a six-two haole transvestite stopping by for a takeout order of the marvelous banana lumpia.

The soups here are quite good; check out the oxtail or the chicken papaya, loaded with ginger and sliced green fruit that gives it an iridescent tint. Pancit dishes are made with rice noodles or egg noodles, and the pusit (squid) adobo is tasty, as are, for that matter, the chicken and pork versions. The pinakbet's terrific, with bits of fried pork, eggplant, okra, long beans, tomatoes, and a dense orange squash similar to pumpkin. A number of dishes are made with either bitter melon leaves or the melon itself, which has an overpowering flavor; it can be omitted at your request. Homemade pickled condiments include mild onions and aspirin-sized chiles that'll blow your doors. No pain, no gain—let that be your mantra.

Pork is dear to Filipinos, and it can be had at Nayong from the hoof upward. Everything from deep-fried pig's feet to an excellent, stew-like gisantes, with chunks of pork, potatoes, peas, and bell peppers in a rich brown gravy. Virtually every dish in the house is between $5 and $6, and portions, though not on the colossal scale of other Filipino diners, are adequate. For dessert, the halo halo ($3) is a must; it's one of the most complex on the island, brimming with everything from avocado to cantaloupe to jackfruit. ♠

Sit-down, simple-fare, low-cost restaurants are important to building community spirit. They are the common man's country clubs, where the affairs of the town get discussed and chewed over...They are, of course, among the many non-chain small businesses which are being pressed into oblivion in our society.
Larry McGehee, syndicated
columnist (1984)

NELLIE'S WHITE QUICHE COMPANY

Maunakea Marketplace #105   CHINATOWN
545-3133   7:30am-5:30pm Mon-Sat
No Plastic   No Alcohol

Quiche
✧

It's certainly reasonable to wonder what, in the name of Pierre Franey, a quiche joint is doing in Chinatown. It seems that proprietor Earnest Sumbry, who named the place after his grandmother, decided on the location simply because "it's the most interesting neighborhood on the island." Though this may seem a tad naive from a business standpoint—after all, quiche ranks right there with crumpets and aerosol cheese in terms of familiarity to most Asians—the man nonetheless has a point.

Nellie's isn't what you would call cavernous. It has precisely two tables, both of which together could fit in the enormous oven Sumbry uses to bake his yolkless pies (hence the term *white quiche*). The menu consists of whatever he has made up that day, usually two or three selections using ingredients like spinach, Maui onion, pesto, curried chicken, tofu, and shrimp. There's always at least one meatless choice, and slices run about $3.50. The quiches are without exception exceedingly attractive and delicious, the two-inch filling smooth and firm yet almost creamy, nestled into a sturdy whole wheat crust. Entire pies are also available, as are fresh baked loaves of Embry's faintly sweet hula bread. ♠

An egg is always an adventure: it may be different.
Oscar Wilde

NEW DALISAY CAFE

1169 Maunakea Street   CHINATOWN
537-6012   8am-10pm Daily (more or less)
No Plastic   No Alcohol

Filipino
✧

There's something decidedly Third World about this dark and muggy place, with its brown and white, unadorned stucco walls, faded orange booths, and veneer tables. The impression is only enhanced by napping children, a long-defunct jukebox, a wobbly gumball machine, and beads dangling in the kitchen doorway. Though they speak little English, the folks here exhibit a common Filipino fondness for American country music—further evidence that sorrowful tunes like "You Picked a Fine Time to Leave Me, Lucille" need no translating.

New Dalisay's menu, a crudely fashioned plastic sign on the back wall, lists a handful of Filipino mainstays—chicken adobo, pinakbet, pancit, dinardaran, pork and shrimp sari sari, and the tangy, tamarind-based soup known as sinigang. These are authentic and consistently tasty, all priced at $5.50. Servings are hefty, and come with a huge wooden crock of rice; even for heavy hitters, polishing off the works can be an arduous task.

While you dine, the clacking of billiard balls wafts in from the Mai Le pool hall across the street. If you're feeling lucky, head over and test your mettle against the local sharks. Or you may want to head around the corner to Randy's Barber Shop on lower Hotel Street, home of the $5 no-refund haircut. ♠

Dinner, a time when...one should eat wisely but not too well, and talk well but not too wisely.
Somerset Maugham

NISSHODO CANDY STORE

1095 Dillingham Boulevard (Building I-5)	KALIHI
847-1244	7am-4:30pm Mon-Fri
	7am-3pm Sat
No Plastic	No Alcohol

Mochi
✧

It's downright amazing the number of sweet and savory items that can be made from mochi, or pounded glutinous rice. As with many a culinary discipline, the Japanese raised mochi processing to an art form, transmuting it into candies and snacks that run the gamut in terms of texture, appearance, and taste. And whether you've been eating the stuff all your life or are just gearing up for your first sampling, you might as well go with the best—in Hawaii, at least, that means Nisshodo.

Not that you'd necessarily get that feeling by looking at the place. Tucked away in a warehouse near Honolulu Community College, Nisshodo isn't exactly high-profile. This is where they make the goods you'll find in stores around town, but they also have a small room where they do the retail thing. A bell rings as you enter, and shortly thereafter someone appears from the factory area. The arare, or mochi crunch, is somewhat pricey ($2.50 for a quarter pound sack) but it's absolutely terrific, with well modulated soy and seaweed overtones. Otherwise, items of interest include monaka, delicate and flowerlike with a thin wafer exterior and sweet bean filling. Also, check out the habutai mochi, poofy domes filed with sweet azuki and dusted with soy powder, or the yaki nanju, dainty bagel-shaped cakes filled with black beans. Perhaps wildest of all are the kin gyo ku, which are bright reds and greens and have a translucence similar to gelatin, but they are much

133

firmer, with a spicy lima bean filling. The goodies here may not be for every taste, but if you're into it, you won't find them any better, anywhere. ♠

Boiled rice doesn't grow on trees.
Japanese proverb

ONO HAWAIIAN FOODS

726 Kapahulu Avenue   KAPAHULU
737-2275   11am-7:30pm Mon-Sat
No Plastic   Bring Your Own

Hawaiian
✧

This is perhaps the most celebrated dispensary of Hawaiian food in the state, with lunchtime lines a common occurrence. Despite the popularity, Ono has over the years made few concessions to its star status, though they display more than a few autographed photos of other luminaries—actor Richard Chamberlain, surfing legend Duke Kahanamoku, the guy who played Oddjob in *Goldfinger*—most of whom have some connection to the Islands. The atmosphere in this small, 10-table eatery is otherwise characterized by shell leis and oodles of red Naugahyde.

As per the custom, Hawaiian food is served as complete plates that include jerkylike pipikaula, lomi lomi salmon, either rice or poi (day-old's better than fresh, with a pleasant tang similar to that of yogurt), and haupia for dessert. The main dishes are either lau lau, kalua pig, or an excellent chicken long rice that's more souplike than most. All of these cost around $6, plus or minus a buck or so. If the aforementioned plates aren't talking to you, Ono's a la carte possibilities are many. Both the chicken and squid luau can always be counted on, as can the beef curry, the poke (fish or squid), and most any of the fried fish items. They do a big takeout business, but keep in mind that to-go lau lau orders must be made a day in advance. ♠

134

> *The taro root looks like a thick, or, if you please, corpulent sweet potato, in shape, but it is of a light purple color when boiled. When boiled, it answers as a passable substitute for bread.*
>
> **Mark Twain**, Mark Twain in Hawaii
> (1866)

ORIGINAL PANCAKE HOUSE

1414 Dillingham Boulevard   KALIHI
847-1496
1221 Kapiolani Boulevard   ALA MOANA
533-3005

                                                      6am-2pm Daily
VISA, MC, AMEX   No Alcohol

Breakfast
❖

Depending on your personal preferences, it may or may not seem a delicious bit of irony that, despite the names, Original Pancake's egg dishes are far superior to those at Eggs 'n Things, while it's vice versa as far as regular pancakes go. Omelettes here are as fluffy and light as you'll find, big feathery pillows stuffed with fried potatoes and crumbled bacon, locally made Portuguese sausage, or just about anything else you might want. All come with three pancakes on the side; though these aren't much count, the specialty pancakes are a different story. Check out either the Swedish or Mandarin translations, the latter referred to here as "the crepe suzettes of the Orient."

Some of the waitresses are German, thick-accented frauleins who if consulted will likely steer you toward a couple of house specialities: the cinnamon-tinged German apple pancake ($7.50), and the eggy, baked pancake known as a Dutch Baby ($5.75). These take about half an hour to prepare but both are splendid, so be patient. This being Hawaii, OPH also offers several plate lunch specials, which you needn't investigate. It's a breakfast place, plain and simple: remember that, and you'll be rewarded.

The interior is basically a half-hearted attempt at the Good Ol' Days motif: lots of varnished wood and stained glass, with a smattering of false needlepoint, synthetic flowers in old soda bottles, and Franklin Mint-type curios. A gilded bald eagle sits above the kitchen door of the Kapiolani location, and there's a passel of

135

decoupage pieces bearing precious adages like "There are no strangers here—only friends we haven't met." ♠

An omelet so light we had to lay our knives across it and even then it struggled.

Margaret Halsey, With Malice
Toward Some (1938)

PAK'S KOREAN KITCHEN

1380 S. King Street   PAWAA
942-8634/941-4218   8:30am-1am Daily
VISA, MC   Alcohol Served

Korean
✧

At first inspection, Pak's appears to be heavily into the yakiniku thing. All the perimeter booths have gas ranges built in, with huge gray exhaust hoods looming above like storm clouds. Upon closer examination, however, you'll probably notice that the majority of folks are slurping some kind of stew or soup, of which there's a heady selection. Pak's big menu also includes sashimi and barbecue plates, but generally speaking the truly great items here arrive in either a bowl or a mini-cauldron—and if one of the lovely muumuu-clad waitresses warns in splintered English that something's hot, you best believe her.

Soupwise, their ample, potent broths (all in the $6-$7 range) come laden with everything from beef stomach to sea bream to yellow corvina. The chicken and green onion soup is quite divine; ditto on the clam version. A far cry from chowder, this, with tofu, chrysanthemum greens, daikon radish, green onions, zucchini and clams aplenty, all swirling in a sweltering broth. Stews are of an equally high caliber, also spicy, steaming, and made with the likes of various fishes, kim chee, tofu, squid, crab, small beef intestine, and on and on. Something for everybody, a credo also embodied in the meal's accompaniments: usually seven or eight dishes containing kim chee (yes, it's as fiery as it looks), pickled daikon, seaweed with chile and toasted sesame seeds, fried tofu covered in sweet catsup, namul, sweetened black soybeans. There's always a different lineup, and it's all as authentic as you'll find. Also worth mention is the unusual green onion jun, made with scallions and small succulent oysters pressed together in a sexy egg pancake.

136

Decor consists of red carpet and burnt-orange booths, with all the counters upholstered in thick white padding that lends a not unpleasant *Superfly*ish aspect. Most everything is in the $6.50-$9.50 range, with noodles a buck or two less. The Korean proclivity for TV in the workplace is displayed, as are the number for Pony Taxi, a large wall calendar, big mirrors, and ads for Korean liquors. ♠

He was a very valiant man who first adventured on eating of oysters.
Thomas Fuller

PARADISE CAFE

66-443 Kam Highway   HALEIWA/NORTH SHORE
637-4540   9am-6pm Daily
No Plastic   Bring Your Own

Vegetarian
✧

Though barely an hour by car, Haleiwa is in many ways a world apart from Honolulu. The town itself is a pleasant, sometimes curious mix of serious surfers and rural-minded locals. It's both more hippiefied and less Asian-influenced than the city, and many of the restaurants here reflect the difference in sensibilities.

With it's neo-wholesome grinds and understated surroundings, Paradise has *North Shore* written all over it. Tucked away in the back of Celestial Natural Foods, they cater mostly to local vegetarians. Though they do use dairy items, the entire back page of the menu is devoted to a summation of the evils—gastrointestinal, moral, and otherwise—of consuming animal products. At any rate, the offerings here are pretty basic: hummus and baba ghanouj are both tasty, and there's also chapati wraps and some hot-dish daily specials, though these aren't much of a deal. The sandwiches are a more satisfying way to go, mostly robust combinations of cheese and veggies, and they also make a tofu spread that's worthwhile. Opt for soup over salad when given a choice. The smoothies are fruity, non-yogurt versions; if you feel

137

your pipes need cleaning, you can get a dash of spirulina added to that for an extra 50 cents. ♠

Most vigitaryans I iver see looked enough like their food to be classed as cannybals.

Finley Peter Dunne, Mr. Dooley's Philosophy (1900)

PENNY'S LUNCH WAGON

205 Sand Island Access Road   KALIHI
845-6503   5:30am-3pm Mon-Fri
                                               6am-3pm Sat
No Plastic   Bring Your Own

Plate Lunch
✧

Welcome friends, to the Hawaii you never see in the travel brochures. Lower Kalihi and Sand Island are the smoky, high-revving guts of an American city, with nary a lei stand in sight. A blue collar atmosphere means blue collar grinds, and Penny's has that in spades. In fact, their plate lunches are a cut above the usual nonsense, easily ranking in Oahu's uppermost echelon.

Prices hover in the sub-$5 range, and selections include excellent stews (beef or curry—either one works), shoyu chicken, sweet-and-sour spareribs. There are also a few surprises like pork adobo, as well as good fried fish (mahi always, sometimes ahi as well). Fridays they serve up a fierce Hawaiian plate: $5.95 gets you an ono lau lau, plus beef stew, some of the better kalua pig around (smoky and moist, without being salty or mushy), lomi salmon, terrific pickled Maui onions, and poi, which can be had sour if you ask. They also serve breakfast, as well as assorted items like pie, manapua, burgers, saimin—plates are the thing, though. Penny's is located just inside a warehouse that also houses a strip bar; besides your car, the only place to sit is an enormous picnic table in the garage area, outside and to your left. ♠

Eat until the lips protrude.
Hawaiian proverb

PEOPLE'S CAFE

1300 Pali Highway   DOWNTOWN
536-5789   10:30am-7:30pm Mon-Sat
No Plastic   No Alcohol

Hawaiian

✧

Like most other places on the island serving decent Hawaiian food, People's has been around for decades and is something of an institution. It's one of the only places downtown offering the real deal, and you can opt for either an a la carte arrangement or one of the combination plates, which are a better deal even though they run toward the high side at $8-$10. Possible options include chicken long rice, lau lau, and kalua pig: the one dish you want to be sure and sample is the squid luau, which is definitive. It's dark green and almost creamy, with a faintly sweet coconut touch. What's more, the squid is perfect, without a trace of rubberiness. Though the menu makes no mention, they'll let you substitute it for chicken luau (also good) on the combination plates. Poi is extra thick one-finger stuff served with onions and rock salt, and the pipikaula is also distinctive—less like jerky, more like pan-fried tenderloin. Ono.

Things move at a relaxed pace here, and during the afternoon lull folks from the neighborhood often drift by to sip coffee and talk a little story with the ladies cutting vegetables in the dining room. Things stays cool thanks to the eternal A/C, and the setting is described by Naugahyde booths and a large refrigerator loaded with poi, lomi salmon, sodas, and a frightful drink called Chocolate Soldier. On the walls are terrific black-and-whites of old Oahu, including taro farmers working their patches and a 1920's sedan tackling the formidable grade of the Old Pali Highway. There are a few spaces in the parking lot beneath the building; otherwise you're on your own, and it can be a bear. ♠

A little taro green is delicious when love is present.
Hawaiian proverb

PHILIPPINE MINI MART

94-871 Waipahu Street   WAIPAHU
677-8181   7am-5pm Daily
No Plastic   No Alcohol

Filipino
✧

Were it not for a large sign announcing the availability of Filipino faves like crispy pata (pig's foot), longaniza (spicy sausage), and chicharon (fried pork skin), all made fresh daily, you'd quite likely float on by, mistaking this place for simply another quick-stop peddling smokes and sodas. And that's if you chanced to be driving in the looming shadow of old Waipahu town's dilapidated sugar mill at all—not likely unless you live here, as the main drag for those passing through is the numbingly dull Farrington Highway.

This is actually a full-on Filipino grocery, albeit in miniaturized form. Every last centimeter of shelf and refrigerator space is jammed with the likes of canned sardines, dried jackfruit, bagoong (fermented fish paste), long beans, mangoes, banana sauce and the like. What with all the cooking, it feels as if you're standing in someone's ridiculously overstuffed kitchen. Some of the crew here speaks modest English, so you may find yourself simply pointing and nodding. They sell balut by the tray (non-Filipinos tend to be less than enchanted by these fertilized duck egg snacks), and they crank out some mighty fine sweet things: flan, a killer halo halo for $2.50, assorted mochi concoctions. Especially keep an eye out for something called puto bumbong. This is made from sticky rice so purple it's almost black, steamed atop a banana leaf and sprinkled with sugar and fresh coconut—a simple but extremely delicious treat, it sells for $2. Check it out. ♠

A great step toward independence is a good-humoured stomach.
                    Seneca

QUINTERO'S

1102 Piikoi Street   PAWAA
593-1561   11am-3pm, 4:30pm-10pm Mon-Fri
                                        4:30pm-10pm Sat-Sun
VISA, MC   Bring Your Own

Mexican
✧

Though the prices certainly can't compete with those in the barrio—$10 looks decidedly more like a floor than a ceiling here—Quintero's offers meals that rank with those at El Charro Avitia as Oahu's premier Mexican repasts. And given the reality that food of this caliber at true bargain prices is about as rare a commodity in Hawaii as moosehide mukluks, it's best to embrace quality and suck it up a little, moneywise.

Quintero's extensive and pleasantly eclectic menu is divided into sections—soups, appetizers, seafood, "birds and fowls"—each headed by a brief and often enigmatic paragraph. "Mexico is the only place in the world where the universal idea of soup does not apply," begins one, while another offers an explanation of the importance of turkey in Mexican culture and cuisine, though only chicken dishes are listed on the menu—the mole sauce, by the way, is excellent.

Mexican Appetizers are in fact full meals, complete with rice and beans, and feature basics like tacos, tostadas, chile rellenos, burritos. You'll also find delicious tortas de papa, otherwise known as potato pancakes, made with eggs, cheese and spices. At around $9, they're one of the cheapest items on the menu. Quintero's also does a nice steamed fish and a spiffy surf-and-turf equivalent (Mar y Tierra) which combines grilled steak, bacon, and shrimp with fresh veggies ($14 or so). The chips and salsa are first-rate, but go easy as meals here are frequently behemothic. Slake your thirst with an agua fresca—the tamarind is particularly fine, less sweet than the others. ♠

The appetite grows by eating.
Francois Rabelais, Gargantua

RADA'S PIROSCKI

1146 Fort Street Mall
533-2388

DOWNTOWN
8am-7pm Mon-Fri
8:30am-5:30pm Sat
9:30am-3:30pm Sun

No Plastic

No Alcohol

Piroscki
✧

Rada's is an excellent example of the fascinating cultural and gastronomic cross-pollination one frequently finds in Hawaii. To wit: Rada's is operated by Filipinos, but their claim to fame is the Eastern European meat-filled buns called piroscki. A sort of over-sized cousin to the Asian manapua, or bao, piroscki are much more dense, and instead of being baked or steamed they are fried to a pleasantly crunchy deep brown. Rada's offers three different fillings, and the saucy beef and cheese with cabbage or the chicken/cheese/mushroom are both prime. These run $1.40 per, a tremendous bargain when you consider their mass—one's enough for most folks, and anyone who downs more than two should head straight for a thyroid specialist. Incongruous though it may seem, the only other item available is a $1 bag of fried squid—sprinkle on some vinegar and a little hot sauce and you're in business.

The lunch special, which costs all of $3 and seems to be obtainable any time of day, consists of a piroscki, squid, and a small tossed salad. Beverages include canned ice coffee, lychee juice, and soy bean drink. The interior's nothing more than a few stools and a stack of local Filipino newspapers—better to find a bench out on the mall, where invariably there's an entertaining cast of characters filing past. ♠

What the sick man likes to eat is his medicine.
Russian proverb

RAINBOW DRIVE-IN

3308 Kanaina Avenue
737-0177
No Plastic

KAPAHULU
7:30am-9pm Daily
No Alcohol

Plate Lunch

The meat and starch coalition known as plate lunch is about as uncomplicated as a meal can get, and it either works for you or it doesn't. If so, then Rainbow's worth knowing about, as it garners con- sistently high marks from connoisseurs of the form. The parking lot, bor- dered on one side by a row of mango trees, is routinely packed with mixed-plate pounding locals, plus a few way- faring tourists out to explore the forbid- ding fringe of Waikiki. The aged building is finished in the sort of smooth green tiles that elicit memories of swim- ming pools and elemen- tary school cafeterias. Across the street is the Ala Wai Golf Course, reputed to be the busiest in the world.

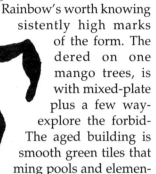

Most everything here falls into the Standards category, with prices hovering around $5. Fried mahi, chicken, hamburger steak, gingery teri beef—expect all of these, plus beef stew or curry beef on Monday, Wednesday, and Friday. The closest thing you'll find to exotica is pork long rice, which shows up a couple of days a week. Rainbow also offers sandwiches ($1.50-$2) and burgers, which can be heard frying somewhere inside premises that are jammed with boxes, buns, and mildly irascible employees. They don't ac- cept $100 bills, and the bathroom key's attached to a plastic gallon jug, lest you have any notions of adding it to your collection. ♠

The flavor of frying bacon beats orange blossoms.
E.W. Howe

RAMA THAI

802 Kapahulu Avenue	KAPAHULU
735-2789	5pm-9:30pm Daily
VISA, MC	Alcohol Served

Thai
✧

The food at Rama Thai compares favorably with most other Thai eating houses on the island, though the menu is somewhat unique in the number of dishes offered bearing a discernible Chi- nese influence. Besides Siamese standards like fragrant curries and mee krob, they offer their own interpretations of borrowed favorites like shrimp in black bean sauce and cashew chicken (excellent, I hasten to add). All this notwithstanding, the most noteworthy feature of the place is the all-you-can-eat buffet on Wednesday nights, which runs about $11 and usually draws a crowd. It's the only one of it's kind around, and seeing as Thai meals often tend toward the Lilliputian the price tag is more of a deal than it may initially sound. Obviously, this carries far greater appeal for serious eaters, though the potential for sampling an array of Thai dishes at once is not without its allure. The buffet menu varies, but typical offerings include decent spring rolls, a noddle dish of some sort (usually pad thai), a vegetarian offering or two, lime-ginger beef that's nigh on excellent, and tapioca for dessert. The atmosphere is pleasant enough, and the service is usually quite attentive. ♠

Eat enough and it will make you wise.
John Lyly, Midas (1592)

RAY'S CAFE

1190 Smith Street   CHINATOWN
536-3392   7:30am-6pm Sat-Th
No Plastic   No Alcohol

Breakfast
✧

Ray's kitchen is dominated by a large open grill, the flames licking and leaping between some of the heftiest beef and ham steaks yet introduced into the modern breakfast equation. The enormity of these meats is at once correlational to the eaters they attract, and in inverse proportion to both the prices and the size of the establishment itself. Measured in ham steaks, Ray's is roughly eight-by-eight, with four small tables. Breakfast-time lines are the rule, and the menu consists entirely of meats—steak, ham, mahi, bacon, Spam, and sausage of several varieties—served with rice and eggs. Otherwise there's shoyu and Tabasco, and that's it—you want frills or a Lite menu, you better look elsewhere. This is Island-style breakfast at its most hardcore; come strong, or don't come at all.

The morning meal is served until 10:30 a.m., after which the menu changes to sandwiches, the aforementioned meats now reposing on a bun. They also have some plate lunch options and a couple of Filipino dishes. Business is steady and the burly clientele is 100% local—cops, construction workers, truck drivers. Aside from the dimensions of their meats, Ray's is most notable for their prices—excepting the steak and eggs, which is probably their best dish and insanely cheap ($4 and change), everything at breakfast is around $3, and lunch is a buck or two more. ♠

Say!
I like green eggs and ham!
I do! I like them Sam-I-am!
And I would eat them in a boat.
And I would eat them with a goat...
And I will eat them in the rain.
And in the dark. And on a train.
And in a car. And in a tree.
They are so good, so good, you see!

Dr. Suess, Green Eggs and Ham

ROYAL VIETNAM

1127 Maunakea Street   CHINATOWN
524-1486   10am-10pm Daily
VISA, MC, AMEX   Alcohol Served

Vietnamese
✧

Far more than a simple pho shop, Royal Vietnam presents a bill of fare considerably more eclectic than those of their counterparts. Among the uncommon offerings are crispy chow mein and magnificent hot pots, cooked with bean sprouts, mint, and lemon grass, and served with all the necessaries for making rice paper rolls. Pricey but impressive, they run about $15 for the seafood combo. In addition to catfish in a number of forms (the braised catfish in black pepper gravy is the one to get), other unusual entrees here include barbecue quail and froglegs fried in butter.

Hot and sour soup (sometimes called hot and spicy) is all the rage in South Vietnam, and it's a big seller here. Thanks to a tamarind-based broth, it's a mind-blower and off the graph in terms of pucker factor. And they do offer pho in a number of guises, including the less commonly seen pho ga, elsewise known as Vietnamese chicken soup. The seafood soups, meanwhile, are compelling assemblies of squid, shrimp, and crab claws, though they run a bit shallow for serious appetites.

The bun dishes are very good and probably the largest in town, with the spring roll/barbecue pork combo especially enticing. Finally, the French influence in Indochina reveals itself in the fondue—thin slices of beef dipped in broth tinged with tamarind, ginger, and lemon grass, then rolled in rice paper with noodles and herbs and dipped in a sweet sauce. Mighty elegant, mighty delicious. In general, dishes run a shade more than the average Vietnamese place, checking in at around $6.50 to $9. Best of the desserts is the coconut milk pudding.

Like their near neighbor, A Little Bit of Saigon, these folks aspire to a more upscale ideal than most of the competition. The ornate interior is long and narrow, rife with reds, greens, and vast mirrors. In the middle of the dining area's a miniature Buddhist temple built onto a support column in treehouse fashion, and that chubby little ceramic figure with the lit cigarette in his mouth is none other than Buddha himself. ♠

There is no such thing as a pretty good omelette.
French proverb

RUBY BAKERY AND COFFEE SHOP

119 N. Hotel Street	CHINATOWN
523-0801	6:30am-10:30pm Daily
No Plastic	Bring Your Own

Cantonese

✧

As Chinatown diversifies and the number of Chinese restaurants in the neighborhood dwindles, Ruby shines ever brighter as a source for superior Hong Kong-style pastries, as well as freshly prepared and preposterously cheap Cantonese fare. The $6.50 crispy-skin duck represents the extravagant end of the menu, with the vast majority of items lagging at least a couple of bucks behind. Excellent dishes like squid with seasonal vegetables (broccoli, onion, carrot) can be had for around $4, and a plate of choy sum with oyster sauce is less than $2. In general, opt in favor of chicken and seafood over beef and pork (though the char siu is a shining exception to this); noodles are also excellent, the chow fun in particular.

The setting is similar to most of the Chinese eating houses in the neighborhood—a bit run-down, perhaps, but honest, comfortable, and frequently bustling. Menus are unbelievably tattered and worn, the tables draped with pink tablecloths, the walls festooned with neon-orange "SPECIAL" signs trumpeting Shanghai noodles and Cantonese rice soup (jook). Baked goods are in the glass case by the door, and most everything is gone by early afternoon. Prices are around 50 to 75 cents per item and there are no duds, but pay particular heed to the curry donuts and anything made with coconut or lemon. If any remain, you must lay claim to one of the incredible lemon rolls—yellow sponge cake wrapped around a thin layer of tangy lemon preserves. ♠

They passed around candy before dinner; it was a regular welcome party. The few Hawaiian workers passed around salt. Chinese take a bit of sugar to remind them in times of bitter struggle of the sweetness of life, and Hawaiians take a few grains of salt on the tongue because it tastes like the sea, like the earth, like human sweat and tears.

Maxine Hong Kingston, China Men
(1980)

SAIGON CAFE

1831 Ala Moana Boulevard	WAIKIKI
955-4009	6:30am-10pm Daily
VISA, MC, AMEX	Alcohol Served

Vietnamese

Waikiki has a way of coercing restaurants, particularly small ones, into compromising their ethnic integrity in an attempt to please everyone. An omnipresent example of this unfortunate phenomenon is the dirt-cheap American breakfast offered by many of the neighborhood's less expensive Asian eateries. Saigon Cafe is one such establishment; in addition to eggs and pancakes they offer a few plate lunch items, all of which you should ignore for what I would hope are obvious reasons. The Vietnamese menu, mean-

147

while, is extensive. First courses to consider are the fried squid stuffed with pork, crab, and shrimp, and the minty chicken salad. Though they have decent pho as well as a continental-inspired crab and asparagus concoction, the hands-down soup of choice is the hot and sour. This brew deviates from its Chinese forebear in all but name, with a disparate, palate-teasing ingredient list that includes tamarind broth, fresh tomatoes, shrimp, sprouts, and pineapple.

The Vietnamese sandwiches here are lofty and superb, with even the most elaborate rendition costing less than $3. The perfect accompaniment to these are the $2 shakes—smoothies, really, made with milk, a few ice cubes, and loads of fresh fruit. The pineapple and papaya shakes are stellar in their own right, but the soursop version will bring you to your knees, its flavor like a coconut-inflected blend of tropical fruits.

Situated amid a cluster of T-shirt and tattoo shops abutting Hilton Hawaiian Village, Saigon Cafe can be tough to find. The carpeted interior is virtually never crowded and actually quite pleasant, with a vaulted wood ceiling and whirling fans. In one corner is a small prayer offering—three cups of tea, illuminated by an electric candle. ♠

"But the chowder; clam or cod for breakfast men?"
"Both," says I, "and let's have a couple of smoked herring by way of variety."
Herman Melville, Moby Dick

SAIGON'S

3624 Waialae Avenue   KAIMUKI
735-4242   10am-9pm Mon-Sat
VISA, MC   Bring Your Own

Vietnamese

France's forays into Indochina weren't exactly anybody's idea of a picnic, but they did result in the birth of one hell of a sandwich. Saigon's are both the biggest and, along with those at Mai's Deli, best in town, competitively priced in the sub-$3 zone. Their French bread, which is delivered each day in huge plastic bags, is the perfect tool for the job: it's tall and slightly chewy, neither crumbly nor too airy. All of the filling options—an assortment of roasted meats, cooked tofu, and pate—are first class. In addition to the pickled celery, carrot, and daikon radish, they add chile sauce, a sprig or two of coriander, and a sprinkling of fried onion bits. The finished product comes wrapped in wax paper secured with a rubber band-pair one of these with an iced coffee and you're sitting fat.

For whatever reason, this place changes names periodically, though everything else seems to remain the same. And while the sandwiches are definitely the bee's knees, they also offer excellent pho and other soups, as well as some elaborate and tasty plates, with nothing much over $5. Crispy fried noodles with seafood is a solid choice, as are any of the rice plates, which are decent-sized and impressively delivered (the best of these is probably the barbecue chicken), with salads of lettuce, tomatoes, cukes, and pickled carrots. Also, try the squid with vegetables or the bun topped with chopped spring rolls. With the exception of lace tablecloths, the setting here is rather minimalist. Notice the large glass counters which seem to serve little purpose other than to house large pans of crushed peanuts, which are sprinkled on practically everything. ♠

There are only two questions to ask about food. Is it good? And is it authentic? We are open [to] new ideas, but not if it means destroying our history. And food is history.

Giuliano Bugialli, New York Times (1984)

SANOYA RAHMEN

1785 S. King Street	PAWAA
947-6065	11am-3am Daily
No Plastic	Bring Your Own

Japanese Noodles

✦

Though fairly inconspicuous by day, one would be hard-pressed to pass down King Street in the wee hours without noticing Sanoya Rahmen. Most of the restaurant's front is glass—a savvy move on the proprietor's part, as it's thus hard to miss the dozens of noodle-minded folks chomping away long after the sun is gone.

The menu is similar to that at other Japanese noodle houses—Ban Zai, Dai Ryu, Tentekomai—though a dash more creative. Besides standard soup noodles matched with the likes of char siu, spicy mabo tofu, and gyoza (all of which are excellent), they also offer some rarely-seen and beautifully rendered alternatives. The chicken vegetable rahmen is sublime, as is the clam version; better still is the Sanoya Special, made with pork, seafood (lots of octopus), and mixed vegetables in a powerful broth that's far spicier than the standard shoyu or miso bases. It runs about $6 (most everything here is in the $5-$6 range), and comes in a bowl deep enough to double as the setting for a Jules Verne tale. Other options include cold noodles and yakisoba (fried noodles), as well as six types of donburi (meat and vegetables over rice), which are tasty but on the small side. The interior has a bright, kind of neo-Tokyo atmosphere, and the kitchen's open, allowing you to see the dour but talented cook in action. ♠

Be as wary of a beautiful woman as you would be of a red pepper.

Japanese proverb

SAU DUONG

58 N. Hotel Street   CHINATOWN
538-7656   9am-9pm Mon-Sat
                                                              9am-3pm Sun
No Plastic   Bring Your Own

Vietnamese
✧

Chinatown is replete with odd cultural juxtapositions, and Hotel Street, with it's strip joints and great restaurants, is Ground Zero in this regard. Sau Duong is but one of many Vietnamese eateries to appear in the neighborhood in recent years, most all of them good at minimum. Out on the sidewalk you may encounter strange dudes lurking in doorways, but step into Sau Duong and the atmosphere quickly changes. Most everyone you see slurping pho or chomping on the fantastic shrimp rolls is Vietnamese, and one gets the distinct impression that they don't eat here because they wandered out of a peep show with an appetite. They come here because the food is consistently good, the portions ample, the price right.

Despite China's profound impact on the cooking of Southeast Asia (all of Asia, for that matter), Sau Duong is one of the few local Vietnamese eateries offering Cantonese-inspired items. These tend to be outstanding if a jot subtle—dishes like stir-fried squid with snow peas, carrots, mushrooms, and bamboo shoots in a light sauce. They also know the way with seafood: shrimp dishes in particular are consistently impressive. The papaya salad here also jams—it's listed as fine-sliced papaya, which is really just another term for shredded. Also expect to find standard items like rice plates and bun topped with grilled pork or chopped spring rolls, served with the usual assorted herbs and accessories.

The kitchen is small and tidy, as is the dining area—basically a few plants, a few mirrors, a few tables. There's rarely a crowd and the service is exceptionally amicable; it's also an excellent place to ask general questions about Vietnamese cuisine, as the staff's English fluency far exceeds the neighborhood average. ♠

Walk 300 paces after meals and you will keep the doctor away.

Chinese proverb

SEKIYA'S

2746 Kaimuki Avenue

732-1656

No Plastic

KAPAHULU

8:30am-11pm Tue-Th

8:30am-12am Fri-Sat

8:30am-10pm Sun

Bring Your Own

Japanese
✧

Despite the proximity to Waikiki, the clientele here is mostly local. It's essentially a Japanese diner, with screen doors in front and a mini-garden complete with bulging carp out back. The inside is as unpretentious as the outside, with booths lining the walls and a jukebox that runs the range—everything from Hawaiian standards to rap.

Dinners feature dishes familiar to anyone who's eaten at Japanese meal-in-a-bowl joints: vegetable tempura with rice, sukiyaki, tonkatsu. Full meals include rice, tsukemono, green tea mixed with roasted barley, and a sweet and surprisingly filling miso soup loaded with tofu. The house special oyako donburi (a sweetish, omelettey

151

concoction of chicken and long rice noodles served over rice) is on target, as is the sukiyaki. The beef tomato is tasty as well, served in an alarmingly huge green plastic bowl. Sekiya's noodle dishes ($3-$5) enjoy an ardent following and are cheaper by a few bucks than the full dinners. Check out the crisp wun tun, the chilled hiyashi somen (slender rice noodles), or the fat and sassy udon. Saimin has become increasingly scarce in anything but the most underwhelming of forms, but Sekiya's treats it in a more exalted manner, with satisfying results. This is also one of the few places you'll find ozoni, the traditional mochi soup. Conversely, they offer a number of American-style sandwiches, and desserts aren't the sort you might expect, either: banana splits, milkshakes, even a Coke float. No kidding. ♠

The American restaurant is never merely a place to eat. It is a place to go, to see, to experience, to hang out in, to seduce in, and to be seduced.
John Mariani, America Eats Out

SHIROKIYA

Second Level   ALA MOANA CENTER
973-9111 (main switchboard)   9am-9pm Daily
VISA, MC, AMEX   No Alcohol

Japanese/Bakery

✦

If Ala Moana Center is one of America's busier shopping centers, it also has to be considered one of the most interesting. In the retail sense, at least, this is the point of maximum contact in the convergence of East and West, and no visit is complete without a stop at Shirokiya, a full-blown Japanese department store. Here, besides fancy electronics and ostentatious jewelry, you'll find a variety of foodstuffs sufficiently dizzying as to necessitate a full afternoon for browsing and snacking. They peddle everything from sushi to grilled swordfish and mackerel, fresh-roasted chestnuts to manapua, baguettes to a vast assortment of green teas. This place is an utter blast, and guest chefs from Japan are frequently flown in to demonstrate esoteric cooking skills of one form or another.

The second-floor bakery is impressive and usually bustling. They have everything from coconut turnovers to curry pies to pineapple-cream longjohns; sweet potato danishes, you'll notice, sit adjacent butterflake donuts that melt on impact. There's also the soft white bread favored by Japanese—brought straight from the oven in loaves so uniformly rectangular they look like stage props—as well as sourdough French and pain aux noix (walnut bread).

Upstairs it's a free-for-all, especially during midday, with free samples of mochi snacks, cuttlefish, wasabi peas, shiitake mushrooms, crunchy soy beans—the list goes on. They also have many prepared items (made here, most of them before your eyes) like marinated kelp and kanago, a salad made with hundreds of little fish (iriko), all tiny and shiny and blended with soy sauce and sugar. There are also small and delicate taiko yaki, Japanese cakes filled with custard or sweet red beans, and Okinawan doughnuts, which resemble a dense fusion of hushpuppy and cake doughnut. ♠

I myself'd gotten the water from the stream, which was cold and pure like snow and the crystal-lidded eyes of heaven. Therefore, the tea was by far the most pure and thirstquenching tea I ever drank in all my life, and it made you want to drink more and more, it actually quenched your thirst and of course it swam around hot in your belly.

"Now you understand the Oriental passion for tea," said Japhy. "Remember that book I told you about the first sip is joy the second is gladness, the third is serenity, the fourth is madness, the fifth is ecstasy."

Jack Kerouac, The Dharma Bums
(1958)

SHUNG CHONG YUEIN

1027 Maunakea Street   CHINATOWN
531-1983   6am-5pm Mon-Sat
                                             6am-2pm Sun
No Plastic   No Alcohol

Chinese Bakery
✧

This is the most revered Chinese bakery in Chinatown, if not the city. Located on a bustling block, the doors are always flung open during business hours, the windows chocked with treats from the Orient. Such is the visual appeal of the merchandise here that

153

there always seems to be someone standing outside gawking. Subjects of these longing stares include all manner of cookies—some flaky, others dense, made with coconut, black sugar, sweet black

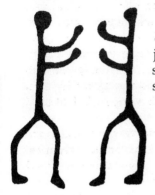

beans, peanuts. Almost all are substantial and delicious, running on the order of 40-50 cents apiece. Don't leave without trying the jin dui—a golfball-sized delight lined with sticky rice and coconut and coated with sesame seeds. It's the best in the city.

Also prominently displayed is a truly exotic selection of dried and candied fruits and vegetables: water chestnuts, mango, papaya, carrots, lotus root, kumquats, ginger, squash and yam, which is especially ono. Something for everyone, and they all go for around $4-$5 a pound—dirt-cheap by my calculations. They also sell mammoth manapua and other savory snacks like fresh-boiled peanuts. Off to one side is a small but significant crack seed selection. Prices tend to be approximated here, toted up on an old manual adding machine and frequently rounded down in your favor so as to avoid making change. Definitely worth a visit. ♠

Food is our common ground, a universal experience.
James Beard, Beard on Food
(1974)

SIAM ORCHID

1514 Kona Street	ALA MOANA
955-6161	
1050 Ala Moana Boulevard	ALA MOANA
591-1199	
11am-2pm, 5:30pm-9:30pm Mon-Fri	5:30pm-9:30pm Sat-Sun(hours vary)
VISA, MC, AMEX	Alcohol Served

Thai

Location notwithstanding—the Kona Street location is hard by the dark and forbidding parking structure of Ala Moana Center—Siam Orchid clearly aspires to a high level of ambience and sophistication. The interior is spiffy, perhaps even elegant, with mauve tablecloths and walls, and plenty of artworks, mirrors and glass brick. However upscale the environs, though, prices are in line with most Thai places around town, appetizers and main dishes mostly hovering toward the low end of the $6-$9 range. Siam Orchid gets some local votes for the best Thai food in town; though one trip to Thai Taste should dispel any such notions in your own mind, the food here is of considerable merit. The extensive selection of first courses includes green papaya salad, spring rolls, satay and fish cakes—all excellent bets. Also compelling are the deep-fried tofu with peanut sauce and the soft and unusual long rice salad, blessed with liberal doses of chile and fresh mint.

The curries here aren't bad but are a shade overpriced, as is the pad thai. Stick instead with the meat and vegetarian categories, where you'll find winners like Evil Beef, Thai-style charcoal-grilled chicken, and panang vegetable and tofu, featuring peanut sauce and blaring sweet basil. Spicewise, they try and err on the side of mildness, which can end up tasting more like Chinese food than Thai. Ergo, any desires you have for even moderate heat must be enunciated. ♠

A good eater must be a good man; for a good eater must have a good digestion, and a good digestion depends upon a good conscience.
Benjamin Disraeli

STORTO'S DELI

66-215 Kam Highway   HALEIWA/NORTH SHORE
637-6633   10am-5pm Daily
No Plastic   Bring Your Own

Sandwiches

It seems rather unlikely—and if you happen to live in Honolulu proper, rather unfair—that the North Shore would be home to two of the best sandwich shops on the island. Such is the case, as Storto's and Kua Aina are separated by nothing more than the thin gray ribbon known as Kam Highway. Proximity notwithstanding, Storto's covers a sandwich aspect left untrodden by Kua Aina: the sub, a.k.a. hoagie, hero, torpedo. Aside from the Detroit Deli, this is the only place on Oahu where you can find the sort of serious, footlong, fully dressed sandwich that make Eastern cities worth saving.

155

There's nothing fancy about the presentation, nothing hoity-toity about the surroundings. These are honest sandwiches for honest appetites, made with sturdy, chewy bread that bears up like a Clydesdale under a load of meats, cheeses, dressings, lettuce, tomatoes, sprouts, onions, mustard, mayo. Subs come either half or whole (roughly $4-$8), with rotating daily specials for about 50 cents less. Mavericks can prescribe their own, otherwise there are standards with local names like Alli (pepperoni/pastrami/ salami), Haleiwa (salami/pepperoni/bologna), Waimea (ham/turkey/salami). There's a choice of six cheeses, and unless you say otherwise they come with the works. Storto's is attached to a surf shop—*everything* on the North Shore is attached to a surf shop—and atmosphere is non-existent beyond Billabong stickers on the door. You can dine outside on the little lanai, otherwise its takeout. Nothing bogus about it. ♠

I told them that I was globally ranked in surfing events, and that I could surf Oahu's six-foot surf with a sandwich in one hand and a Marlboro in the other.

Barry Williams (a.k.a. Greg Brady, on lies he told *The Brady Bunch* producers), Growing Up Brady (1992)

TAJ MAHAL

1309 Kalakaua Avenue
947-4729

VISA, MC

PAWAA
11:30am-2pm, 5pm-9pm Mon-Fri
5pm-9pm Sat-Sun
Bring Your Own

Indian

✧

Honolulu has never had to wrestle with the question of how to deal with an overabundance of good Indian restaurants; in fact, the recently opened Taj Mahal has been a welcome bright spot on a heretofore bleak corner of the local culinary landscape. The owners are from various regions of the home country (one is actually Pakistani), and their menu's a successful attempt to cover multiple facets of Indian cooking. The South is represented by a number of fine curries, made with either chicken or lamb. The chicken tikka masala—boneless morsels of bird, first barbecued and then bathed in a moderately spicy tomato gravy—is fabulous, the meat so incredibly tender as to be almost spreadable.

The chief cook, meanwhile, is from northern India, land of the tandoor, or clay oven—an apparatus which he clearly knows his way around. In fact, Taj Mahal turns out a top-notch tandoori chicken that rates with any you'll find on the Mainland. Devoid of both excessive heat and the sort of mealiness that results from over-marinating, it's a brilliant red, lean and succulent with a pleasant charcoal twinge.

For vegetarians, there are a number of delicious curries, among the best of which is the aloo gobhi: cauliflower and potatoes cooked with herbs and spices, tinged with a pleasant sweetness. The dal, however, isn't up to the level of the other items. Given that entrees lurk around $10, the all-inclusive $9.95 dinner buffet is a bargain and the $6.95 lunch version is an extraordinary deal. There's a rotating assortment of curries and chicken dishes that offer plenty in the way of options for carnivore and vegetarian alike, plus fresh-baked naan that's slightly resilient and wonderful. As with many an Indian cook, these guys aren't averse to whipping out the salt shaker; luckily, they're equally unreluctant to lay on some heavy spices—plan on healthy and recurrent blasts of saffron, cardamom, cumin, coriander, pepper, cinnamon, mustard seed, and anise.

The atmosphere is definitely not why you come here. Think of it as American Insurance Office, circa 1970: unadorned walls stretching up to a 20-foot ceiling, covered with off-white, prefab paneling and paper of a green that adjectives fail to capture. There is exactly one plant, and it tends to be rather warm in here, so be sure to dress accordingly. ♠

He who plants a coconut tree plants vessels and clothing, food and drink, a habitation for himself, and a heritage for his children.

Indian proverb

TAMASHIRO MARKET

802 N. King Street
841-8047

PALAMA
8am-6pm Mon-Fri
9am-6pm Sat
9am-4pm Sun
Alcohol for Sale

No Plastic

Seafood/Poke

✧

Now that they no longer sell their trademark coconut pudding, Tamashiro's seems more focused than ever on transporting seafood poke to new and exhilarating heights. They take the stuff very seriously, as they do all things oceanic; housed on the ground floor of a three-story, pink building festooned with an enormous crab, their sign exclaims, "Most Complete Seafood Store," a declaration that's hard to dispute.

To the left of the entrance is a large and detailed fish chart, to the right an article detailing the benefits of devouring our gilled buddies whenever possible. The store itself isn't all that large, its narrow aisles jammed with fresh ginger, sliced papaya, seafood, people, and more seafood. The central segment of the store is topped by a scaled-down hull of a Japanese fishing vessel, complete with portholes. The entire back of the store is devoted to poke— an enormous glass display case filled with 25 different kinds, everything from mussels (about $5 per pound) to crab. The ahi options are legion (check out that wicked kukui nut variation). The most glorious and colorful style, when available, is made with large pieces of sweet, succulent surf crab, onion, sliced red and green peppers, and enough chile flakes to make things interesting. Such is the beauty of this concoction that at first glance it looks like some tropical fruit salad, and the sweet/hot/ocean flavor is simply unimprovable. Poke isn't meant to be pounded in mass quantities, and a quarter-pound tub is enough for one person to have a nice snack. Tamashiro's makes it fresh almost continuously, and they recently added some terrific smoked ahi to their list of offerings. This is also an excellent source for ahi steaks, daikon kim chee and crabs, kept in gurgling tanks on the far side of the store. The staff's a little on the brusque side, but they know their fish. ♠

The real native South Seas food is lousy. You can't eat it.

Victor "Trader Vic" Bergeron,
Newsweek (1958)

TANIGUCHI STORE

2065 S. Beretania Street
949-1489

MOILIILI
8am-6pm Mon-Sat
8am-5pm Sun
(last bentos made around 2pm)

No Plastic

Alcohol for Sale

Bentos

✧

Here stands a definitive example of a dying breed, the Japanese family-owned neighborhood store. While others succumb to competition from the big boys, evil developers, or simple decrepitude, Taniguchi rocks on.

Immediately upon entering what appears from the outside to be your garden-variety market, you'll find, displayed just below the cartons of cigarettes, a rather amazing assortment of bentos—things like spicy fried chicken wings, several kinds of sushi and musubi, chilled noodles, and fried whole fish. Everything runs in the $3 range, give or take; if you can't find anything to interest you, proceed around the store's perimeter to the kim chee and other pickled vegetables, chilling in large buckets. Or mosey toward the back—past the tubers and roots, the bananas hanging on hooks, the fat Kahuku papayas—where you'll find whole dried fish, still more pickled items, curry croquettes, vegetable tempura and crispy spring rolls for under a buck.

Taniguchi's is a neighborhood place, surrounded by small businesses and boxy, cinder-block apartment houses. Traffic is steady all day, much of it Asian ladies from the area come to peruse the goods and chat up their friends working the registers. Out front are beautiful ginger plants for sale, above which swing weathered paper lanterns advertising Yamasa Soy Sauce. ♠

Eating is heaven.
Korean proverb

TEDDY B'S

136 Wilikina Drive
621-SOUL (7685)

No Plastic

WAHIAWA
11am-10pm Th-Sat
1pm-8pm Sun
Bring Your Own

Soul Food

❖

Quite understandably, soul food isn't something most people associate with Hawaii. Much of the Islands's black population is concentrated around the military bases, the largest of which is Schofield Barracks in Wahiawa—otherwise notable as the setting for the film *From Here to Eternity*. There are actually two soul food places in the state (the other being Mr. Turner's), and they are both located here, on the same short street.

The owners are originally from L.A., the children of Southern migrants who brought their culinary traditions with them. The food here is consistently excellent, with entrees such as catfish (very good), chitlins (Friday and Saturday only), barbecue ribs, and fried chicken wings. Somewhat alarmingly, meat offerings typically out-number vegetables: the collard greens are very high grade, and the yams are tasty as well, shot through with clove and cinnamon. There's also macaroni and cheese, and occasionally black-eyed peas, garlic-laden in a way they never are down South. Different but delicious, better still with a shot of hot sauce.

There are two kinds of people in this world—those that make cornbread with white meal, and those that make it with yellow. Virtually all cornbread served outside of Dixie is the sweet, cakelike yellow version you'll find at Teddy B's. Desserts include Sock It to Me Cake, peach cobbler, and sweet potato pie (the filling is identical to the aforementioned yams). The lone drawback to Teddy B's is the price: everything's a la carte, with most entrees over $10 and veg-etables and desserts about $2 each. Even cornbread's extra, so be prepared. Teddy B's is spacious and nicely decorated, with matching tables and chairs and plenty of ceiling fans. By far the most notable feature of the decor is the hundreds of album covers adorning the walls, virtually all by black recording artists—

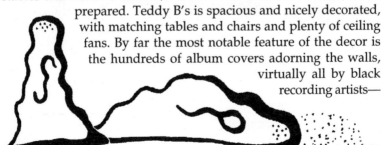

everybody from Sly and the Family Stone to Donny Hathaway, Miles Davis to Richard Pryor. There's live jazz on Sundays from 2 p.m. to 5 p.m. ♠

- Avoid fried meats, which angry up the blood.
*- If your stomach disputes you, lie down and pacify it
    with cool thoughts.*
*- Keep the juices flowing by jangling gently as you
    move.*

Satchel Paige

TED'S BAKERY

59-024 Kam Highway   HALEIWA/NORTH SHORE
638-8207   7am-6:45pm Daily
No Plastic   No Alcohol

Bakery
✧

Like D'Amicos Pizza next door, Ted's caters to the surfing crowd, a congregation quite capable of appreciating shabbiness and good chow in equal measure. Ted's is essentially a cramped one-stop market, though they also dabble in plate lunch and sandwiches. These you can take or leave, but not so the baked goods.

Ted started out baking with the big hotels, and he adroitly learned all aspects of the trade prior to bailing for the country. Now's he's got his own gig, and the Sunset Beach crowd is that much the richer for it. Though the danishes and muffins at Ted's are certainly passable (skip the brownies, though), serious players will want to check out the monster cakes—selection varies, but watch for lemon, buttercream, German chocolate, or guava—and the pies, of which the coconut cream and the macadamia nut are not to be missed. ♠

---

*More people will die from hit-or-miss eating than
from hit-and-run driving.*

Duncan Hines, Adventures in Good
Eating (1936)

TED'S KIM CHEE TO GO

2820 S. King Street   MOILIILI
946-0364   10am-9pm Daily
No Plastic   Bring Your Own

Korean/Plate Lunch

✧

As the name intimates, there's no indoor seating at Ted's: just a kitchen, a window through which business is transacted, and a flock of outdoor tables should you wish to stick around. This is first and foremost a Korean takeout joint, but they also offer a number of local plate lunch items. The Korean portion of the menu features standard fare, mostly barbecued meats and tasty man doo—small stuffed dumplings, in this case deep-fried. As is the ritual, all meals are served with rice and fiery kim chee (wedged into little paper cups), as well as cool, marinated watercress and sesame-soaked bean sprouts. Meals are large and generally quite the bargain, running in the $4-$5 range; the specials and the combination plates are usually the way to go. Another item of interest is the barbecue beef sandwich, topped with kim chee, oddly similar to North Carolina-style barbecue—if that means anything to you—only much hotter. Ted's also sells kim chee by the pint, quart, and gallon. ♠

There is no such thing as a little garlic.
Anonymous

TENTEKOMAI

2126 Kalakaua Avenue   WAIKIKI
922-3583   11am-1am Daily
No Plastic   Alcohol Served

Japanese Noodles

✧

The Japanese tend to be a serious people when it comes to noodles, and they harbor a particular fondness for the thin wheat noodles known as rahmen. And despite the unencouraging address and the $1-$2 premium (expect to pay $5-$7.50) that goes with it, this place ranks with the best noodle houses in town. The menu is small, the service good, the clientele almost exclusively Japanese—in fact, many Japanese tourists who visit Tentekomai are sufficiently impressed so as to snap photos of one another standing before the picture menu. The place itself is easy to miss, near Fort DeRussy in a small, inconspicuous retail cluster that's also home to a Harley Davidson clothing shop and the Skin Deep Tattoo Parlor. Nonetheless, it's decorated with unusual taste and discretion for this zip code, with a tile floor, sliding doors that are always open, and a terrific wraparound wood counter wide enough for parking your Toyota.

Rahmen's served nine different ways: the standard version is broth with plenty of noodles, seasoned pork, and bamboo shoots of unsurpassed quality, quite apart from the pithy planks you may be used to seeing. The most popular dish in the house is the rahmen/gyoza combo, perhaps because the gyoza (veggie and pork dumplings) are outstanding, a more delicate cousin to the Chinese pot sticker. Other dishes to bank on are the cold rahmen, the paicoh, which is topped with a fried pork cutlet, and the umeboshi, made with seaweed, bamboo shoots, and the same pickled plum you find in sushi rolls. It's not for everyone, I grant you, but damn tasty if you're feeling open to a little adventure. ♠

While two are eating, one would not know even though the other should die.
Korean proverb

THAI TASTE

1246 S. King Street   PAWAA
526-3772   11am-2pm, 5:30pm-10pm Daily
VISA, MC   Bring Your Own

Thai
✧

Forget all the propaganda you've heard about Keo's being the Thai food standard-bearer in Hawaii; it exceeds Thai Taste only with regard to price. Despite the lack of notoriety, this is home to the best Thai food in the state, hands down. It's a laid-back, family operation (though all you ever see is women and children) with an unassuming exterior that gives way to an exceedingly pleasant interior, characterized by the conscientious use of pinks, lots of painted paper fans, and photos of Thai royalty. Definitely not run-down, but not self-consciously fancy, either; just comfortable and relaxing, the sort of place for lingering your way through a meal.

163

Thai restaurants tend to have standardized menus, with dishes like pad thai, spring rolls, Evil Beef, and coconut-lemon grass soup available anywhere and everywhere. Thai Taste has all that, but they also demonstrate a beguiling willingness to veer from the standard playlist. Witness the likes of crab curry, sour red curry made with pork and ong choy, and vegetarian delicacies like deep-fried papaya for $5. Or perhaps the Eggplant Smoothie—slightly disconcerting nomenclature, true, but the union of sliced green eggplant, Thai basil, and tender boneless chicken in a dark, chile-sprinkled sauce has a way of obviating any urge to be critical.

The appetizers, soups, and salads are all worth serious investigation, with nary a pretender in the bunch. Watch for their landmark version of mee krob, a sweet, crispy noodle salad; springy, fried fish cakes with minced long bean; Tiger Tail Salad, made with thin-sliced barbecue beef; and nam prik, a shrimp paste ground with garlic, chiles and lime juice, then eaten with eggplant fritters, ong choy, poached squid, or damn near anything else. To the adventurous gourmand, these are the things that make life worth living. Unlike virtually every other Thai restaurant in Hawaii, Thai Taste offers up portions that actually warrant the adjective *substantial*. What's more, their prices rank at the bottom of the scale, with the vast majority of entrees priced below $6 (excepting the seafood, which is also relatively cheap). Thai Taste has the cheapest sticky rice in the city, and $1.50 buys either Thai iced coffee or homemade coconut ice cream topped with gooey palm seeds and crushed peanuts. It's not uncommon for them to be out of something, and equally likely that they'll honor special requests. ♠

If you slaughter a buffalo, don't spare the spices.
Thai proverb

THANH BINH CAFE

590 N. King Street   IWILEI
845-5360   8am-9pm Daily
No Plastic   Bring Your Own

Vietnamese

Thanh Binh epitomizes the sort of scruffy, easy-to-miss Vietnamese eateries sprinkled throughout Chinatown, though it's actually about a half-mile away. It's a quirky place where prices are ridiculously low, the staff amiable and often eager to know how you found them. The dearth of English fluency here manifests itself in interesting ways: the menu can be difficult to decipher ("beep noodle soup"), and the small TV is as likely to be tuned to low-budget televangelism as *Macneil-Lehrer*. The decor, meanwhile, is an amalgamation of elements seemingly gathered from food service establishments gone by—mismatched tables, stick-on mirrored tiles, even a small ice cream counter that seems to have been moved with each visit.

To the seasoned cheap eater, of course, idiosyncracies like these add up to one huge All Systems Go, and those who go to the trouble of finding Thanh Binh won't come away disappointed. Besides pho, bun, and an absolutely killer bo tai (marinated beef salad), they take great pride in a number of more unusual offerings. Things like mock duck, made with thin strips of fried tofu, or the Special Pan Cake (elsewhere referred to as a Vietnamese crepe), made with eggs, flour, coconut milk, sprouts, and shrimp, meant to be rolled and dipped.

The $1.55 fruit shakes are a revelation, and this is the only other place on the island besides Saigon Cafe that serves a soursop version, though they don't necessarily tell you that's what it is. Overall, prices float pleasantly in the $5 range, with many items considerably less. ♠

Today's patron is more sophisticated than in the past and recognizes items of value on the menu. Failure to change prices as product and labor costs change may encourage patrons to take advantage of prices advantageous to them...

Jack E. Miller, Menu Pricing and Strategy

TO CHAU

1007 River Street   CHINATOWN
533-4549   8am-2pm Daily
No Plastic   Bring Your Own

Vietnamese

To Chau has a reputation for serving Hawaii's premier bowl of pho, and the accolades are well-deserved, indeed. In fact, so confident are the owners in their ability to turn out superior product that they serve pho and little else.

Crowds are common here and the tables large, so when the line is snaking down the sidewalk you may end up sharing table space with strangers. Most patrons are Vietnamese, and English is an infrequent ingredient of the cacophonous banter. There are a couple of appetizers—including absolutely fabulous rice paper rolls, hearty and cheap, served with a dipping that oozes peanut/hoisin nuance—and a few rice plates which no one ever orders. Soup's king here, and it comes in three sizes ($4-$5). There are 14 combinations; one of the specialties is thin slices of raw beef, supple and pink, served on the side. These are to be dropped directly into the steaming broth, an event preceeded by much doctoring with chile sauce, white pepper, fish sauce, and the like. Rare-steak alternatives include meatballs, tripe, brisket, flank, and tendon. Any or all, the price is the same and the experience memorable.

Though orders are taken and food delivered in a timely fashion, things here seem to be in constant upheaval. One of the main players is a bony gentleman who can usually be seen rushing about in manic procedures, shouting directions in Vietnamese. The guy's in constant motion; customers, meanwhile, hunch and slurp as if there were no tomorrow. As you might well expect, atmosphere is pretty straightforward: ceiling fans, red chairs, white tablecloths, fake paneling. The doors are always open and—get ready for a shock—iced coffee is the drink of choice. ♠

The sense of smell is especially effective in arousing memories.

Schopenhauer

TONKATSU JUGEMU

1960 Kapiolani Boulevard	McCULLY
943-8873	5:30pm-9:30pm Daily
VISA, MC	Alcohol Served

Japanese
✧

Tucked inconspicuously behind the stairs in a nouveau mini-mall, this place seems a little slicker on the inside, with nice woods and fancy tables taking the place of the usual particle board and formica. As with most Japanese eating-houses serving neither sushi nor Kobe steaks, the menu here is small; atypically, however, it's presented on a large wooden tablet shaped like a pig. Main points of interest are donburi (meat and rice in a bowl, topped with curried eggs and onions), and things like chicken cutlet, tonkatsu, and fried potato croquettes, which are superb and remarkably similar to a potato knish. Specialty of the house is pork fillet tonkatsu, though the regular tonkatsu is actually more flavorful. The fried squid excels as well. Plates are a bit high, starting at around $8.50 and ascending to $13.50 for the Mixed Fry. Though portions are modest, meals come with unlimited rice and bottomless miso soup (excellent stuff it is, loaded with daikon and tofu). The one notable exception to the fry-happy approach is the pork ginger—thin-sliced, piquant, and real, real fine. Wash everything down with cups of splendid genmai-cha, a green tea blended with roasted, popped rice. In the middle of each table sits a monster crock of homemade tonkatsu sauce—tangy-sweet and flecked with dark sesame seeds. Most patrons are Japanese, many of them from the I'm-naked-without-my-cellular-phone school of restaurant-going. ♠

Bad dinners go hand-in-hand with total depravity, while a well-fed man is already half saved.
The New Kentucky Home
Cookbook (1884)

TROPICAL RUSH

59-254 Kam Highway   HALEIWA/NORTH SHORE
No Phone   Morning to Afternoon Daily
No Plastic   Bring Your Own
Smoothies/Sandwiches
✧

According to their literature, Tropical Rush is sponsored by the Church of Hawaiinei as part of an effort to promote native Hawaiian health centers. To all outward appearances, though, this is simply quintessential North Shore commerce: take a sky-blue stepvan, put in a sliding glass window, park it roadside between Pipeline and Sunset, add a few picnic tables and a shelter in case it rains, and brah, you got a restaurant. And you can't miss it, either, thanks to the 20-foot wooden statue next door.

As befits an eatery equipped with four-on-the-floor, the menu is simple and geared for takeout. Breakfast is a bowl of cereal, a

waffle with fruit, or poached eggs and toast, all in the $2.50 to $4.75 range. After 11 a.m., you're looking at good cheap sandwiches on whole wheat (avocado and cheese for $3.75, tuna salad $2.75) or vegetarian chili with brown rice. A side of fruit salad goes for two bucks and change. Smoothies are a big draw; all contain bee pollen and honey, combined with banana, pineapple, papaya, or guava. Lovers of the unusual may be aroused by the peanut butter version, which isn't as cloying as you're thinking and actually pretty decent. The Hawaiian is a better choice, made with fruit and poi, which is essentially undetectable—it's refreshing, though really more of a beverage than a true smoothie. Smalls can be had for around $1.75, larges for $2.50. ♠

Do not waste food lest Haloa (the taro god) turn around and stare.

Hawaiian proverb

VERBANO

3571 Waialae Avenue	KAIMUKI
735-1777/735-1778	11am-2:30pm, 5pm-10pm Mon-Sat
	5pm-10pm Sun
VISA, MC, AMEX	Alcohol Served

Italian

✧

Even with a recent price boost, Verbano remains one of the best Italian food bargains on Oahu. The atmosphere is conducive to both romance and good digestion, the service pleasant and without pretense, and the meals routinely fantastic.

The lighting in here is subdued, so sit near the front windows if your eyesight's at all shaky as the menu's worthy of a serious browsing. For a first course, skip the salads and opt for one of the 14 appetizers. The carpaccio is excellent (fresh raw steak, sliced whisper-thin and served with onions, horseradish and capers). The roasted peppers with anchovies is also superb (about $6), while the stuffed peppers alla kubosan (made with seasoned homemade breadcrumbs, garlic, and olive oil) is the deal of the lot at under $4. Entree prices here can prod the edges of the cheap-eating envelope, but many dishes come in two sizes, the smaller of which is usually quite ample. Pastas are consistently good, and besides the standard alfredos, marinaras, and primaveras, there are beguiling options like linguini pesto or arrabiata, a tomato sauce made with bacon, ham and garlic, served over penne or rigatoni. You'll also do well to try the homemade cheese ravioli. Other dishes of import include a righteous and filling chicken saltimbocca (made with eggplant, mushrooms, butter, wine, and cheese), and the seafood ravioli in a creamy pesto sauce. If you've made peace with the idea of eating veal, they handle that nicely, too—try the cheesy, eggplant-studded provencale. The bread here is good and they keep it coming, and desserts include a warm and velvety zabaglione for around $3. Non-meat-eaters are well provided for, as vegetarian pasta dishes outnumber meaty ones. Expect to lay out $7-$10 for pasta, a couple of bucks more for most everything else. Yet another good place to eat in Kaimuki. ♠

To lift off the cover of a tomato-y mixture and let it bubble up mushroom and basil under my nose does a lot to counteract the many subtle efforts a part of me makes to punish myself for all those worst of my shortcomings—those I can neither name nor find a shape for. Terrible brown ghosts with sinews like bedsprings.

Mary Virginia Micka, The Cazenovia Journal (1986)

VIET HUONG

3565 Waialae Avenue
732-4507

VISA, MC, AMEX

Vietnamese

KAIMUKI
10:30am-9:30pm Mon-Sat
5pm-9:30pm Sun
Bring Your Own

Block for block, Kaimuki's one of the few neighborhoods blessed with enough restaurants to give Chinatown a run for its money. Along with Hale Vietnam and Saigon's, Viet Huong forms an imposing triumvirate of Southeast Asian eateries that few areas can match.

Viet Huong is a monument to the Vietnamese proclivity for understatement, and despite its small sign and the drapes always being drawn, business is steady. Excellent first course items like summer rolls (made with two types of mint leaves), bo tai, and jellyfish salad are likely to draw your eye, but none have the head-turning power of the pineapple salad. $7.50 gets you a sexy conglomeration of shrimp, pork, onions, and chunks of fresh fruit; served in a pineapple half and topped with cilantro, peanuts, and bright red chiles, it looks like something out of a cruise ship ad. Do not fail to order it.

The bun dishes ($6 range) are on the small side but extremely well rendered. Try the beef with onion and lemon grass or the grilled shrimp. Shellfish are always good here, so try the hot and sour soup with shrimp or the fresh-water lobster sauteed with garlic (both around $10) if you're into the little guys. Also excellent are the fondue, any of the crispy noodle dishes, and the chao tom. The latter consists of shrimp paste wrapped around sugar cane, grilled and served with all the necessaries (herbs, rice vermicelli, lettuce) for making rice paper roll-ups. Though a little on the spendy side at $11.50, in terms of both texture and flavor it's a thing of beauty and highly recommended. Though prices here are a buck or two more than most Vietnamese eating palaces, portions are generally hefty and these folks seem incapable of hitting a false note. Order with confidence. ♠

Poor Japhy, it was here I finally found out his Achilles heel. This little tough guy who wasn't afraid of anything and could ramble around mountains weeks alone and run down mountains, was afraid of going into a restaurant because the people in it were too well dressed. I got mad and said, "What you afraid of, Japhy, what's the difference? You may know all about mountains, but I know where to eat."

Jack Kerouac, The Dharma Bums
(1958)

WAH FUNG BINH DAN QUAN

2636 S. King Street

945-3815

No Plastic

MOILIILI

10am-9pm Wed-Mon

No Alcohol

Vietnamese

✧

The owners are a Chinese/Vietnamese couple, a circumstance that's led to some confusion for would-be patrons of this tiny 10-seater near the University of Hawaii. Various signs announce "Chinese Kitchen," "Vietnamese-Chinese Cuisine," and "Vietnamese Food." It's this last one you should take seriously—very seriously, as Wah Fung is one of the best places at this end of town for Saigon-style grinds, and one of the cheapest anywhere on the island.

The $3 shrimp rolls excel, but if you're wanting to spread your wings a bit in the appetizer department try the meat balls, which you wrap in rice paper with Vietnamese basil and cool sprouts, then dip in a sweet vinegar sauce. The beef sa-te salad is also formidable, thanks to the holy trinity of chiles, vinegar, and garlic. Pho fiends might as well order the big kahuna, otherwise known as Special Look Fun Beef Soup (about $5). It has everything—rare and flank steak, bits of tripe, and chewy tendon. Like everything else offered, you'll find a picture of it (number eight, aerial view) in the handy photo album accompanying the multilingual (English, Vietnamese, Chinese, Japanese) menu. They also have seafood soups which are tasty and photogenic, though a bit small.

The atmosphere at Wah Fung is decidedly mellow, and you rarely if ever have to wait for a table. The place itself is showing signs of wear, but I'll take that over high-neon pretense anytime. Mainly it's a few plants, a couple of hand-lettered signs and maybe a stray newspaper or two. Dessert's a simple affair but not to be missed: $1.25 gets you a plastic cup of chilled tapioca coupled with any of a number of interesting partners—everything from banana to mung bean, taro to corn to Okinawan sweet potato, which is purplish and dense but only slightly sweet, great with iced coffee. ♠

When it comes to Chinese food I have always operated under the policy that the less known about the preparation the better...A wise diner who is invited to visit the kitchen replies by saying, as politely as possible, that he has a pressing engagement elsewhere.

Calvin Trillin, Third Helpings (1983)

171

WAH KUNG

2850 Pukoloa Street
833-0880/833-0881
VISA, MC

MAPUNAPUNA
10:30am-9pm Daily
Bring Your Own

Cantonese

✧

Wah Kung is located in what's left of the Gibson's Shopping Center. This place looks deserted (though you'll notice that the rearmost portion of the otherwise empty lot is being used by the Toyota dealership next door), and matters are further complicated by Wah Kung's eschewing any sort of substantial sign, despite being on the backside of the complex facing a huge concrete wall and hence completely invisible from the nearest streets.

So why come to this Mall That Time Forgot, in a neighborhood comprised mainly of warehouses, a few office buildings, and a Jack-in-the-Box? Because the food here is excellent, excellent—most excellent. It's Hong Kong-style, and the menu offers both diversity and deliciosity (which, if it isn't a word, damn well ought to be). Everything's fresh, hot, plentiful, cooked to order, and otherwise groovy in every way. Take, for example, the char siu look fun ($4.50 for a serious pile of food), made with sturdy wide noodles and loaded with julienned vegetables and sweet roast pork. They pride themselves on seafood here, and in addition to the 30 or so offerings on the menu there are usually another five or more specials. These are likely to include items like spicy shrimp in the shell or clams in black bean sauce—especially terrific, thanks in no small part to a homemade sauce that's surprisingly gingery without the usual saltiness.

They do all the little things right here, too—plenty of rice, good tea, and a friendly staff that may express mild surprise you found them, particularly if you aren't Asian. The interior, by the way, is basic Chinese restaurant-style—a large, open room, big tables, ornate ceiling. Check out the murals on the back wall, which feature a perplexed-looking dragon on a leash and fair and tender ladies playing musical instruments. ♠

Given extensive leisure, what do not the Chinese do? They eat crabs, drink tea, taste spring water, sing operatic airs, fly kites, play shuttle cock, match grass blades, make paper boxes, solve complicated wire puzzles, play mahjongg, gamble and pawn clothing, stew ginseng, watch cock-fights, romp with their children, water flowers, plant vegetables, graft fruits, take afternoon naps, have three meals in one, guess fingers, play at palmistry, gossip about fox spirits, go to operas, beat drums and gongs, play the flute, practise on calligraphy, munch duck gizzards, salt carrots, fondle walnuts, fly eagles, feed carrier pigeons, quarrel with their tailors, go on pilgrimages, visit temples, climb mountains, watch boat races, hold bull fights, take aphrodisiacs, smoke opium, gather at street corners, shout at aeroplanes, fulminate against the Japanese, wonder at the white people, criticize their politicians, read Buddhist classics, practise deep-breathing, hold Buddhist seances, consult fortune tellers, catch crickets, eat melon seeds, gamble for moon cakes, hold lantern competitions, burn rare incense, eat noodles, solve literary riddles, train pot-flowers, send one another birthday presents, kow-tow to one another, produce children, and sleep.

Lin Yutang

WAIAHOLE POI FACTORY

Kam Highway at Waiahole Valley Road
239-2157

No Plastic

WAIAHOLE
10am-2pm Fri
(or until the food runs out)
No Alcohol

Hawaiian

✧

Waiahole Valley is as country as it gets on Oahu, and most of the residents are taro farmers. With the assistance of Hui Ulu Mea Ai, a non-profit group dedicated to sustaining small farming and fishing in these economically exasperating times, the taro is processed and marketed via the Waiahole Poi Factory, which also serves as home to a catering business. Lucky for me and you, they go retail for a few hours a week, and the Aloha Friday Hawaiian plates are nothing short of masterful. Simply put, this is one of

173

the most enjoyable cheap-lunch excursions you can make on Oahu.

The half-century-old building is spartan in the extreme; bordered by sugar cane and banana plants, it stays boarded up most of the time. But by 10 a.m. on Fridays there's a sizable line, which usually continues unabated until the food runs out sometime between noon and 2 p.m. Get here early, unless you want to risk stepping up to a "sorry brah, all pau" after 20 minutes of waiting. Lau lau or kalua pig plates are a rock-bottom $3.50, and you can get both for $5.25. The pig is cooked in a nearby imu and it's particularly noteworthy—succulent and uncharacteristically lean, without peer on the island. The poi varies depending on the variety of taro they use (usually mo'i), but it tends to be lighter and milder than most. There are only a few seats at a makeshift table outside, but a jovial mood pervades, so it seems quite natural to be knocking elbows with strangers. ♠

A universal food for natives, poi has not often won the affection of passing visitors, many of whom have hit independently on the same description of its taste, that it is like stale library paste.

Waverley Root and **Richard de Rochemont**, Eating in America (1976)

WAIOLA STORE

2135 Waiola Street
949-2269
No Plastic

MOILIILI
9am-7pm Daily
Alcohol for Sale

Shave Ice

The way Jerry Lee sees it, he's a student, and shave ice is his manuscript. Since his father bought Waiola Store in Moilili from Jerry's great-uncle seven years ago, Jerry has studied the form, learning all there is to know about what constitutes the perfect shave ice (which, by the way, was introduced to the Isles by Japanese immigrants come to work on the sugar plantations). He discovered that texture is perhaps the most critical and difficult-to-modulate elements of great shave ice. When done right, it shouldn't call to mind a snow cone, with which it's often compared by the unenlightened, so much as just plain snow. It should be fine, almost powdery, never chunky. If this sounds like a trivial detail, it isn't. Try the rest and then come to Waiola Store, where the shave ice is always right on the money: smooth and absorbent, not at all crunchy or wet. Despite the low profile, this attention to the finer points of an Isle tradition has won them a loyal following, and on hot days they've been known to plow through upwards of 200 pounds of ice.

There are more than 20 flavors to pick from here, the most interesting being tropical choices like mango, coconut, passion fruit, pina colada, haupia. And you'll definitely need to try the li hing mui, which is made from the same preserved plum found in crack seed shops. The Lee's make the syrup themselves and it's a delectable stroke of sweet, salty genius not to be missed. After your tab is paid ($2 tops), have a seat on one of the benches and go to work. Better still, head around the corner to Old Stadium Park, check out the clouds as they settle along the Koolau, and congratulate yourself on having the good sense to be in Hawaii. ♠

I am beginning to learn that it is the sweet, simple things of life which are the real ones after all.
Laura Ingalls Wilder (1917)

W & M BAR-B-Q BURGER

3104 Waialae Avenue   KAIMUKI
734-3350   9am-4:30pm Tue-Sun
No Plastic   No Alcohol

Burgers
✧

W & M started out on the corner of Waialae and 9th Avenue in Kaimuki more than three decades ago, before moving to the present location in 1980. Though it sits back from the road in the shadow of City Mill, with barely so much as a visible sign, business is brisk thanks to a legion of devoted burgerhounds and a reputation for serving the best.

The setting is a wooden building done up in mock Old West style. There are two walk-up order windows, no seats, and one scraggly poi dog sacked out on a towel in the kitchen doorway. Your choices are charbroiled

175

burgers or thin ribeye sandwiches, both of which you'll smell cooking long before you see them in all their flamekissed glory. Orders are filled with great rapidity, and many patrons simply eat in their cars (parking here is no easy feat) or stand around munching.

Burgers (around $2.50) aren't all that huge, but man they're good. The steak sandwiches ($3-plus), meanwhile, are thin and tender with teriyaki overtones, somewhat messy but never soggy. Try them with mustard, which provides a neat foil for the sweetness of the marinade; this same rationale dictates that you skip the relish. The fries have plenty of devotees, and are similar to the best fast-food versions, thin with crispy tips and served in a paper sack. The only other item besides beverages is the $1.50 Crab-flavored Salad, which we don't even need to discuss. Decor consists of pictures of the old place and several large signs announcing, "We Do Not Accept Any Bills Over $20." Simplfy, simplify. ♠

I hoped to find down the county roads Ma in her beanery and Pap over his barbecue pit, both still serving slow food from the same place they did thirty years ago. Where-you-from-buddy restaurants.
William Least Heat Moon, Blue
Highways (1982)

WONG AND WONG

1023 Maunakea Street   CHINATOWN
521-4492   10am-2am Daily
VISA, MC   Bring Your Own

Cantonese

Located in the heart of Chinatown, Wong and Wong isn't known for it's ambience. The large, open dining room is pretty stark, the walls festooned with dozens of bright, handwritten signs that seem to suggest virtually the entire menu is on special. Up front there's usually an arrangement of fresh pomelos in the window and a large tank containing some menacing-looking fish—pets, presumably. The service, meanwhile, tends to be on the nonchalant side, but the food is usually worth abiding the occasional slight.

Glancing back and forth from walls to menu, you begin to get an idea of the eclectic nature of the offerings here. Selections include decent hot pots (a Cantonese favorite); a vast assortment of seafood dishes ranging from shrimp and squid in myriad forms to pearl abalone w/ mushrooms; and rarely seen dishes such as pepper salt frog legs. Noodlewise they show some impressive chops, and the Hong Kong-style crispy chicken is, in a word, excellent. Portions are average, as are the prices: most everything shows up in the $4-$8 range, with the majority of dishes $6 and under. If you've got plenty of company, check out one of the elaborate group meals— quite the bargain, and enough food to burn up the bearing in your lazy susan. Enjoy. ♠

Cantonese will eat anything in the sky but airplanes, anything in the sea but submarines, and anything with four legs but the table.

Amanda Bennett, The Wall Street Journal (1983)

WOODLANDS

1289 S. King Street
526-2239
VISA, MC

MOILIILI
11am-2pm, 5pm-9pm Wed-Mon
Bring Your Own

Cantonese

Though virtually everything offered at this snazzy eatery is quality merchandise, the snapshot items featured on the inside cover of the menu are superlative. Among the subjects are potstickers, plump and moist with a faintly crisp bottom and plenty of filling. The chicken and chive ($6 or so) rendition is particularly sublime, which is why just about everyone in the place is nibbling an order (the fish and chive gau gee are likewise impressive). Also making love to the lens are black bean chicken fried noodle and the hot and sour soup.

Unlike most versions it goes pretty light on the ginger, but adds a heady sprinkling of fresh coriander leaves. A medium bowl is enough for 3 or 4 people and runs about $6. Unphotographed best bets include eggplant, either in a spicy garlic sauce or stuffed with fish cake and deep-fried. And vegetarians, take note: the stir-fried choy sum is handled with aplomb, not even remotely overcooked. These guys are pros—even the hot tea's unusually tasty and mellow.

In general, prices are a couple of bucks more than most Chinese restaurants in the area, but portions are generous and the atmosphere is a notch above in terms of elegance, what with the crisp tablecloths, expansive mirrors, ornate ceiling, relief art, gurgling fountain and so forth. Parking is in the lot around back. ♠

Please understand the reason why Chinese vegetables taste so good. It is simple. The Chinese don't cook them, they just threaten them!

Jeff Smith, The Frugal Gourmet
Cooks with Wine (1986)

YAKINIKU CAMELLIA

2494 S. Beretania Street   MOILIILI
944-0449/946-7595
930 McCully Street   MOILIILI
951-0611

11am-10pm Daily
VISA, MC   Alcohol Served

Korean Yakiniku
✧

Honolulu is many, many things, but one thing it isn't is a great buffet town. Sure, there are plenty around, mostly in Waikiki, but they tend to emphasize quantity at the expense of quality, with a high price tag being salt in the proverbial wound. Luckily with many a grim rule, though, there's often the luminous exception to keeps us from losing all faith in mankind. Witness, then, Yakiniku Camellia, Hawaii's only Korean buffet and one of Oahu's superlative dining experiences.

The yakiniku (cook-it-yourself) concept is something of a mania in Korea, and it's showcased here to exceptional effect. This Far Eastern approach to strapping on a feedbag seems particularly brilliant in contrast to most American-style buffets; because it takes time to cook your food, you're encouraged to pace yourself and enjoy, instead of bolting everything in sight like some frenzied lab animal. Ergo, you should allow ample time for this meal—say, an hour, minimum, with two better still.

You'll find a clean, well-lit place, with large booths and a gas grill in the middle of each table. Being a Korean restaurant, the emphasis here is on barbecue and kim chee. There are several kinds of fresh, high quality meat, including the ever-in-demand kal bi(short ribs), bulgogi (beef), chicken, and spicy pork. Besides plenty of fresh veggies primed for grilling, there's kim chee by the tubful. About 15 varieties, in fact, all made on the premises—cucumber, daikon, watercress, flaming-hot won bok, chewy tae goo (dried cuttlefish). There's also soup, rice, and garlic and peppers for roasting on the grill. For dessert, there's fresh fruit. In the miserable event that you don't care for barbecue or kim chee, there's a forlorn little salad bar, some passably decent potstickers, and a barely-touched tray of the blandest, whitest fried rice this side of Oriental Night at a North Dakota truck stop. For those up to the job, Yakiniku Camellia is a hellacious bargain, though it's not inexpensive in the strict sense. But as anyone who has ever bought a Yugo can ruefully explain, price ain't everything. Dinner includes sashimi and costs about $14, but the real bargain is lunch, which lasts until 3 p.m. and runs about $9. Camellia is often crowded, especially in summer (it's popular with Korean and Japanese tour groups). So come early, stay late, and remember—no swimming for at least an hour. ♠

He didn't care one way or the other..."so long's we can eat, son, y'ear me? I'm hungry, I'm starving, let's eat right now!"—and off we'd rush to eat, whereof, as saith Ecclesiastes, "It is your portion under the sun."

Jack Kerouac (description of Dean Moriarty), On the Road (1957)

YAMAGEN

2210 S. King Street   MOILIILI
947-2125   11:30am-2pm, 5:30pm-9:30pm Wed-Mon
No Plastic   Bring Your Own

Japanese

✧

The atmosphere at Yamagen's, like the food, is a fitting study in simplicity. So simple in fact that, besides not advertising in the broader sense of the term, they have practically eschewed the notion of a sign altogether, so keep your eyes peeled. The menu

179

features basic Japanese standards without a lot of fanfare, and most meals come with very fine miso soup and a bit of tsukemono. Takeout's available—at lunch, it's all that's available—and they have a tiny but terrific courtyard in back if you want to eat here. Portions are average.

Inside are four tables and a few stools at the counter—again, modest but very pleasant. No matter where you sit, it's almost impossible not to see, hear, and smell the flurry of kitchen activity. Chickens are being deboned, onions chopped, issues resolved. Orders are cooked as they're received, and nothing benefits from the arrangement more than the tempura. Yamagen does an especially stellar job in this area: for between $5 and $8 you can get shrimp and/or squid, plus vegetables—eggplant, squash, green beans, thin-sliced sweet potato—all coated with a light batter and expertly fried, the end product a piping hot, virtually greaseless master-piece. Most everything else is of a similar caliber, particularly the donburi and anything containing the fat and chewy udon noodles. Despite their disdain for precooking, service is usually very fast, particularly at lunch. ♠

Man is born to eat.
Craig Claiborne, Craig Claiborne's Kitchen Primer (1969)

YONG SING

1055 Alakea Street
531-1366
VISA, MC

DOWNTOWN
9am-9pm Daily
Alcohol Served

Dim Sum
✧

This is, and has been for years, one of Honolulu's premier spots for dim sum. It's a vast, cavernous place with a multi-story white exterior accented by a huge arching doorway that's difficult to miss, from land or air. Inside, the bilevel dining area is packed with giant tables well suited to the predominantly Chinese clientele who rarely seem to show up in groups of less than 10.

Dim sum is served from 9 a.m. to 2 p.m. every day, with Sundays drawing the biggest crowds. The orange-shirted waitstaff are masters at taking large orders without benefit of pencil, paper, or abacus, and they also see to it that you're well outfitted with hot tea and hot mustard. As you call out your selections they nod approvingly; if they've run out of something or the chef simply wasn't in the mood, they shake their heads and say "no more." As various items emanate from the kitchen, it's a sight to behold: steamed buns bulging with char siu, Chinese sausage, chicken and black mushrooms, or black sugar; chewy mochi dumplings filled with chicken or coconut (truly outstanding, these); steamed shrimp or scallop gau (mini dumplings); deep-fried taro balls; curry turnovers; and beef shumai. More elaborate items items like braised spareribs, chicken feet in black bean and pepper sauce, and the chicken, abalone, and fish maw roll cost a few bucks each, but virtually all of the baked items and dumplings are less than a dollar. Everything is terrific, and two people can usually dine rather spectacularly for under $15.

If you arrive too late for dim sum, you can still do quite well with the rest of the menu; count on any of the barbecue items being pretty much of a sure thing, and ditto with the duck. Also strong are the hot pots, which at around $7 exceed most of the menu by a couple of bucks but are well worth it. And vegetarians have some nice options here, as these folks really know how to work a vegetable. ♠

In general, mankind, since the improvement of cookery, eat twice as much as nature requires.
Benjamin Franklin

ZORRO'S

2310 Kuhio Avenue   WAIKIKI
926-5555   10am-2am Daily
No Plastic   Alcohol Served

Pizza

✧

An alphabetical listing of superior open-air pizza joints in Waikiki begins and ends with Z. Zorro's is the one chance to do yourself right in the W zone, either with a slice or a whole pie.

The place itself is small and primarily a takeout operation (they deliver as far away as Makiki and Kaimuki), with lots of red and black, neon beer signs, and posters for upcoming T & A contests.

181

The shop is an offshoot of Zorro's in New York; apparently the original Zorro was from Naples, and the pizza here is Neopolitan-style, with a fairly thin crust that's sturdy even at the tip and pleasantly crispy at the edges—perfect for folding in the middle and eating on the fly.

The $1.50 cheese slices sell big, with extra toppings (fresh mushrooms, Maui onion, pineapple, Italian salami, and so on) costing another 50 cents per. Whole pies come in 16-inch only, and run from $11 to $20 as you move along the all-or-nothing gradient. Otherwise, big burly calzones are a deal for $4 and change, as are the similarly priced 7-inch subs, featuring fresh Italian bread stuffed with high-grade salami and mortadella from Scala's in Chicago. On the counter you'll find dented shakers of garlic powder, red pepper flakes and oregano, should you wish to do a little fine-tuning. ♠

Tomatoes and oregano make it Italian; wine and tarragon make it French. Sour cream makes it Russian; lemon and cinnamon makes it Greek. Soy sauce makes it Chinese; garlic makes it good.

Alice May Brock, Alice's
Restaurant Cookbook (1969)

GLOSSARY

AHI — Yellowfin tuna. Frequently used as sashimi or in poke.

ADOBO — A Filipino dish usually made with pork or chicken, simmered in a vinegar/garlic sauce.

AKU — Skipjack tuna. Slightly darker than ahi.

AKULE — Mackerel-like fish, available at Japanese bento counters either smoked or fried whole.

APPLE BANANA — Smaller and spicier than regular bananas.

AZUKI BEANS — Sweetened red or black beans, frequently used in Japanese confections.

BAGOONG — Pungent, salty paste made from small shrimp or fish (usually anchovies). A Filipino staple.

BAO — Chinese name for manapua, or steamed buns.

BITTER MELON — Spiny member of the gourd family, used in Chinese and Filipino cooking. Definitely bitter.

BUTTERFISH — Black cod. Very fishy, often used in Japanese dishes. Also a traditional ingredient in lau lau.

BULGOGI — Korean barbecued beef. Gingery and thin-sliced.

CHAR SIU — Chinese barbecued pork. Somewhat sweet, with a distinctive red tint.

CHICKEN LUAU — Chicken cooked with coconut milk and spinach-like taro leaf.

CHILE WATER — Relatively mild all-purpose condiment found in most Hawaiian restaurants.

CHINESE PARSLEY — see **CORIANDER**.

CHOW FUN — Wide, stir-fried Chinese noodle.

CHOY SUM — Thick-stalked green favored by Chinese and Koreans.

CORIANDER — In Hawaii, this usually refers to the distinctive herb—also known as cilantro or Chinese parsley—not the ground seed. Vital to Southeast Asian and Mexican cooking.

DAIKON — Long, light-colored turnip common in Japanese and Korean dishes. Similar in flavor to a radish.

DIM SUM — Any of a number of Chinese dumplings that are steamed, baked, or fried. Often refers to a style of eating more than specific foods. Literally, "dot the heart."

GISANTES — Filipino dish usually made with pork, tomatoes and peas.

HALF MOON — Dim sum item consisting of translucent dough stuffed with minced meat and vegetables and steamed. Sometimes called sow's ear.

183

HALO HALO — Popular Filipino dessert of evaporated milk (sometimes coconut milk), chipped ice, and a varying assortment of fruits, sweet beans, and miscellaneous doodads.

HAMACHI — Yellowtail tuna. Frequently used for sushi.

HAUPIA — Pudding made with coconut milk and arrowroot.

HOISIN SAUCE — Thick, sweet sauce made from fermented soy beans. Common in Chinese and some Southeast Asian cooking.

IMU — Traditional Hawaiian underground oven.

JAI — Also called monk's food. A traditional Chinese vegetarian dish consisting primarily of several types of mushrooms.

JIN DUI — Popular dim sum item. Chewy fried balls made with mochi rice and filled with coconut, black sugar, or sometimes char siu.

JOOK — Also called congee. Very bland Cantonese rice soup, usually seasoned with a variety of condiments.

KAL BI — Korean favorite barbecued short ribs marinated in a shoyu/sesame oil blend.

KALUA PIG — Barbecued pork, cooked whole in an imu.

KAMABOKO — Fish cake made from pureed white fish. sometimes tinted pink. Often used in rahmen and saimin.

KARE KARE — Filipino stew usually made with beef, oxtail, eggplant, and green beans in a peanut broth. Served with bagoong.

KATSUDON — Japanese dish of fried pork cutlet over rice, topped with an egg and onion mixture.

KIM CHEE — Korean pickled vegetables—cabbage, radish, greens, cucumbers, you name it—seasoned with garlic, chile, salt, vinegar, and whatever else seems interesting.

LAU LAU — Pork and small bits of fish wrapped in taro leaf (this you eat) and then ti leaf (inedible), then steamed. Sometimes made with beef or chicken.

LI HING MUI — Asian-style preserved plum. Sweet and salty, with a faintly prunish taste.

LILIKOI — Passion fruit. Citruslike, often quite tart.

LIMU — Seaweed used in poke.

LOMI LOMI SALMON — Hawaiian dish made with diced salmon, tomatoes, and onion. Served cold.

LONG RICE — Cellophane noodles made from mung bean flour.

LUMPIA — Filipino appetizer similar to spring roll, only smaller. Sometimes stuffed with banana.

LUP CHEONG — Chinese sausage often found in manapua and other dim sum items. Anise-flavored, faintly sweet, somewhat oily.

LYCHEE — Fruit with sweet, smooth flesh. Grows in the Islands.

MAHI MAHI — Sometimes called dolphinfish. Ubiquitous in the Islands, often fried in batter or sauteed. Flesh is light and firm.

MALASADA — Yeasty Portuguese donut, similar to French beignet. Sans hole and rolled in sugar, they're usually made fresh.

MANAPUA — Chinese buns filled with char siu, black sugar, or oyster chicken, to name but a few possibilities. Usually steamed, sometimes baked.

MAN DOO — Korean stuffed dumpling, similar to won ton.

MARRONGAY LEAVES — Small, rounded leaves of horseradish tree used in Filipino cooking.

MAUI ONION — Mild white onion, with sweetness similar to a Vidalia.

MEIN — Thin Chinese wheat noodle, often stir-fried (chow mein).

MISO — A fermented soy paste used in soups and stews.

MOCHI RICE — Also called sweet, sticky, or glutinous rice. Used to make Japanese rice cakes, sweets, and mochi crunch (arare).

MONGO BEANS — Filipino term for mung beans.

NAMUL — Korean side dish of lightly cooked vegetables sprinkled with sesame oil, vinegar, shoyu, and sesame seeds.

NORI — Thin sheets of seaweed used for wrapping sushi.

OHELO BERRY — Bright red, similar to a huckleberry. Sacred to Pele, the volcano goddess.

OKAZU-YA — Japanese delicatessen.

ONO — Also called wahoo, this fish has firm white flesh and a mild flavor. Occasionally available smoked.

OPAKAPAKA — A pink snapper. Excellent grilled or as sashimi.

OPIHI — Island limpets, sometimes used in poke.

OZONI — Japanese soup traditionally eaten on New Year's Day, made with mochi and vegetables.

PANCIT — Filipino dish made with egg or rice noodles.

PAO DOCE — Portuguese sweet bread.

PASTELES — Bananas stuffed with pork and steamed.

PHO — Delicate Vietnamese beef noodle soup. Typically served with fresh sprouts, herbs, chiles, and lime.

PINAKBET — Filipino dish of simmered vegetables and either shrimp or pork. Eaten with mounds of rice.

PIPIKAULA — Hawaiian beef jerky.

POCHERO — Filipino stew of beef, chicken, dumplings, and vegetables.

POHA BERRY — Very tart, similar to a gooseberry. Frequently used in jams and ice cream.

POI — Staple starch of the Hawaiian diet, made from boiled taro root mashed into a thick, purplish paste. Day-old's tangier than fresh.

POKE — Raw fish or other seafood mixed with items such as limu (seaweed), onion, kukui nut paste, red chile.

POMELO — Citrus fruit reminiscent of a grapefruit only larger.

PORTUGUESE SAUSAGE — Spicy pork sausage, heavy on the red pepper.

PUPU — Catchall term for snack or hors d'ouevre.

SAIMIN — Rahmen-like noodle soup of local invention.

SARCIADO — Filipino dish characterized by tomato sauce and either meat or seafood.

SASHIMI — Any saltwater fish sliced thin and served raw.

SHABU SHABU — Meat and vegetables cooked in simmering broth.

SHIITAKE MUSHROOMS — Broad group of black mushrooms central to Chinese and Japanese cooking. Used dried or fresh.

SHOYU — Soy sauce.

SHUMAI — Small steamed dumplings, also called pork hash.

SINIGANG — Filipino soup made with tamarind, okra, long beans, and meat.

SOBA — Slender Japanese buckwheat noodle.

SOMEN — Very thin and delicate Japanese rice noodles, often served cold.

SOURSOP — Large tropical fruit with creamy white flesh. Tastes like a blend of mango, coconut, and other fruits.

SPAM — The less said, the better.

SQUID LUAU — see **CHICKEN LUAU**.

TAMARIND — Tree that produces pods containing sour pulp, used in Southeast Asian and Filipino cooking.

TARO — Ultrastarchy tuber, a staple of Polynesian cooking.

TEMPURA — Vegetables, meat, and/or seafood quick-fried in a light egg batter.

TONKATSU — Breaded, deep-fried pork cutlet. A popular Japanese lunch item, it's served with a tangy dipping sauce.

TSUKEMONO — Japanese pickled vegetables. Considerably milder than kim chee.

UDON — Thick wheat noodles, popular in southern Japan.

WASABI — Hot, green horseradish paste used in sushi.

WON BOK — Pale cabbage popular in Asian cooking, especially favored for kim chee purposes.

INDEX #1
BY ALPHABET

INDEX #2
BY LOCATION

INDEX #3
BY FOOD

YOU'VE BOUGHT THE BOOK — NOW IT'S TIME TO PUT IN YOUR TWO CENTS.

If by some wild fluke of the cosmos you disagree with our assessments, or you think we've committed grievous sins of omission, we want to hear about it. An updated edition of *Adventures in Cheap Eating*—including the Neighbor Isles—is already in the works, so here's your chance to pontificate. Using the form provided or a reasonable facsimile of your own making, let us know your thoughts, hopes, dreams, recommendations...

━━━━━━━━━━━━━━━━━━━━━━━━━━━━

Hi, my name is:_____

address:_____

_____ phone:_____

Here's what's on my mind:_____

_____

_____

_____

_____

_____

❖ When discussing specific restaurants, please include addresses and phone numbers whenever possible. Thanks, and happy eating.

TSUNAMI PRESS   P.O. BOX 62197   HONOLULU, HI 96839